THE HUMAN MIND OWNER'S MANUAL

An Interactive Guide to the Most Powerful Machine on the Planet: Your Mind!

(Using Psychology, CBT & REBT)

The international best-selling online course, now available as a book!

Joeel A. Rivera, M.Ed.
& Natalie Rivera

Copyright © 2020 All rights reserved.

ISBN 978-1-60166-054-1

FREE ONLINE COURSE!

Flip to the end of this book to find out how to enroll in the FREE online course(s) that bring this book to life!

Plus, learn how to become a Certified CBT/REBT Mindset Life Coach.

CONTENTS

SECTION 1: Introducing the Human Mind Owner's Manual . 7
1: The Most Powerful Machine 7
2. A Human Empowerment Story 10
3. A Brief History of CBT, REBT and Psychology 11
4. Similarities and Differences Between REBT & CBT 15

SECTION 2: The Growth Mindset 23
1: Why the Growth Mindset is the Key to Changing Your Mind .. 23
2: Locus of Control 27
3: Developing a Growth Mindset Step 1: Awareness 31
4: Developing a Growth Mindset Step 2: Perspective 34
5: Developing a Growth Mindset Step 3: Action 36

SECTION 3: How the Mind Works 39
1: Thoughts Create Emotions and Behaviors 39
2: We All Think Irrationally! Yes, even you! 44
3: Cognitive Distortions 46
4: R = Rational: Irrational vs Rational Beliefs 51
5: E = Emotive: Unhealthy vs Healthy Negative Emotions .. 54
6: B = Behavior: Unconstructive vs Constructive Behavior . 56
7: Intellectual vs. Emotive Understanding 59
8: The Three Levels of Thinking 60

SECTION 4: Developing Awareness of Thoughts, Emotions, and Behaviors 63
1: Cultivating Mindfulness and Self-Awareness 63
2: Developing Awareness of Your Thoughts and Self-Talk .. 66
3: Developing Awareness of Your Emotions 71
4: Situational vs. Psychological Fear 75
5: Identifying Triggers 77
6: Identifying Underlying Beliefs 80
7: A Note About Acceptance 84
8: Mindfulness Meditation 85

SECTION 5: Irrational Beliefs and Emotional Disturbances . 87
1: Two Ways We Disturb Ourselves Emotionally 87
2: Evaluative Thinking: 4 Dysfunctional Ways We Assign Meaning   90
3: The 6 Human Needs 93
4: Core Beliefs (Rules and Musts) that Make Us Miserable 97
5: Major Must #1: APPROVAL—I must be approved of by others to be worthy. 97
6: Major Must #2: JUDGMENT—Other people must do "the right thing" and meet my expectations in order to be worthy. 101
7: Major Must #3: COMFORT—Life must be easy, without discomfort or inconvenience. 104
8. Core Belief Identification Chart 109

SECTION 6: The ABCDEF Journaling Process 115
1: Why Journaling is the Core of CBT and REBT 115
2: The ABCDEF Journaling Process 116
3: Simplified ABCDEF Form 119
4: Daily and Weekly Journal Prompts 133
5: Additional Journal Prompts 133

SECTION 7: Steps 1-3 (A, B & C): Identifying Activating Events, Beliefs & Consequences 137
1: A = Activating Event 137
2: B = Beliefs 140
3: C = Consequences 142

SECTION 8: Step 4.1 (D): Disputing Irrational Thinking, Beliefs and Perspectives (Inferences) 147
1: D = Disputing, Part 1—Inferences 147
2: Unconditional Acceptance 149
3: Banish Approval-Seeking and Say No to "Should" 153
4: The Power of Perspective 156
5: Reframe Negative Experiences 159
6: Positive Thinking and Affirmations 162
7: Stop Irrational and Illogical Thinking with Socratic Questioning   164
8: Putting Thoughts on Trial 166
10: Fact or Opinion 167

SECTION 9: Step 4.2 (D): Changing the Meaning You Assign (Evaluations) 169
1: D = Disputing, Part 2—Evaluations 169
2: Changing Your Evaluative Thinking 171
3: Turning Demands into Preferences 172
4: Expand Your Boundaries and Embrace Uncertainty 174
5: De-catastrophizing (Overcoming Worry) 178

SECTION 10: Step 4.3 (D): Disputing Your Core Beliefs 181
1: D = Disputing, Part 3—Core Beliefs 181
2: Challenging Irrational Core Beliefs 182
3: Changing Limiting Beliefs 184

SECTION 11: Steps 5 & 6 (E & F): Determining the Desired Effect, Taking Action & Creating Change 189
1: E = New Effect 189
2: F = Further Action 192
3: Overcoming Indecision Part 1: Autopilot and Being Stuck 195
4: Overcoming Indecision Part 2: Irrevocable Choices 197
5: Overcoming Inaction 200
6: Exposure Techniques for Overcoming Fear and Resistance . . . 202
7: Identifying What You Want 203
8: The Brain Science of Visualization 207
9: Create a Vision of Your Future 209

Meet the Authors 211

Take the Online Course or Become a Mindset Life Coach 212

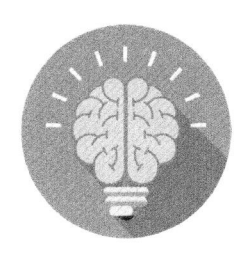

SECTION 1: INTRODUCING THE HUMAN MIND OWNER'S MANUAL

1: THE MOST POWERFUL MACHINE

You were probably never told that you are the owner of the most powerful machine on the planet—the human mind! It is what allow us humans to paint masterpieces, build modern marvels, make scientific discoveries, and learn through books like this one. But, unfortunately, our minds don't come with an instruction manual. Most people never reach their potential because their machines—the most powerful tool they will ever have—inherited faulty programming. But, it's not their fault—they were never taught how their mind works, how to reprogram it, or how much power they have to create the lives they want.

You were probably never taught that you have the ability to change ANYTHING about yourself—your level of intelligence, your talent, your abilities, and your personality.

You were probably never taught that you have the ability to control your thoughts, emotions, and behaviors, and you certainly weren't taught how.

You may have been told you could be or do anything you wanted when you grew up, but you never believed it (and neither did the people who told you this). You were surrounded by people who settled in life, who were unhappy, who were dysfunctional and who, unfortunately, passed the beliefs and patterns of thinking that got them there onto you.

Now you're grown up and you have a million thoughts that run through your mind that make you doubt yourself and believe your dreams aren't possible.

Like most people, you've got a monkey mind that's always negative and distracting you from creating the life you want.

It's time to give your monkey mind a banana. This book is the banana!

This book will teach you how your mind works, including the #1 most important thing you could ever understand about yourself, which is that your thoughts are what create your emotions.

That's right, even though it seems like the situations or people around you are causing you to feel a certain way, the truth is that it is what you THINK about the situation that causes your emotion.

Knowing this gives you your power back because through this book you can learn how to CHOOSE YOUR THOUGHTS. By doing so you can control your emotions and ultimately create your destiny.

But, here's the bad news… this super-computer you have, this human mind, it's flawed. Your thinking has the power to transform your life! But, without training, the human mind is extremely IRRATIONAL and can wreak havoc on your happiness and behaviors.

Our brain's primary objective is to keep us safe. Unfortunately, in its quest to interpret our world and keep us safe it misinterprets what's happening, it makes false judgments, and it demands unreasonable things from ourselves, others, and life. Plus, after years of living around dysfunctional people we pick up their faulty belief systems—mind viruses.

That's why this book is so important!

In this book you will learn how to reprogram your mind and avoid the ultimate form of failure, which is to achieve success in your life but still feel unfulfilled.

This book will teach you the two psychological frameworks that are at the root of modern positive psychology: Cognitive Behavioral Therapy (CBT) and Rational Emotive Behavioral Therapy (REBT). The insights and techniques of CBT and REBT have unlocked human potential in the last century and are what ultimately differentiates those who are successful from those who are not.

You'll learn how your thoughts and emotions work and how to identify why you think and act the way you do. You'll develop self-awareness so you can stop negative thinking in the act and retrain your monkey mind to think more positively and rationally.

You will learn how to rewire your faulty belief systems and stop sabotaging yourself. This book won't just teach you how to use positive thinking to feel better in the moment, it will teach you how to identify the root cause of your emotional pain and rip it out!

Can you relate to any of this?

- Do you ever feel stuck, like you know what you want but you just can't get yourself to do what you need to do?
- Do you ever feel torn between doing what you *really* want and doing what you believe you "should" do?
- Do you ever feel like your thoughts, your emotions, or your life are out of your control?
- Do you ever make irrational decisions you later regret?
- Do you ever feel overwhelmed with stress, worry, and fear of uncertainty and failure?
- Do you have an inner critic that is always putting you down, telling you you're not good enough, and beating you up for mistakes you make?
- Have you ever had the sinking feeling that YOU are the biggest roadblock that is stopping you from reaching your potential?

If so, you are not alone! Welcome to being human. We are all gloriously dysfunctional because we're wielding the most powerful machine on the planet and no one taught us how to use it. It uses US.

That stops today! You're holding in your hands the Human Mind Owner's Manual that you never knew existed.

The good news is that this manual is not like most user's manuals... it is not filled with hard-to-decipher diagrams and grossly mis-translated instructions. It's organized in a clear, logical manner and written in everyday language that an 8th grader could understand.

However, this book is not a Bible. We cannot cover EVERYTHING you could ever need to know to totally grasp everything about the human mind, the brain, and psychology in the however-many-pages-this-book-is book. If you find the way humans think and act fascinating, consider going to college for psychology and/or sociology (we did!). If you want to know more about positive psychology, brain science, life coaching or anything else we talk about in this course, do some research on good-old-Google or nerd-out on some documentaries or online courses (we do!).

The more you know about that mushy-yet-powerful lump of meat in your noggin the more you will want to know. It's interesting and useful! But, we will warn you… once you open Pandora's Box, you can't stuff it back in. Once you take the Red Pill, you can't un-know what you learn. And you won't want to. You might even become obsessed (we are)!

2. A HUMAN EMPOWERMENT STORY

They don't teach this stuff in school. Our parents don't know it either. That's why we're never told about the superpowers of our minds or that we have control over how we think, feel and act. As a result, we tend to spend our lives feeling like the victim of circumstances. Life happens TO us. What we experience in life is determined by the outside world and we have little to no control over it.

Most people believe they're dealt a hand of cards at birth—including the parents card, the community card, the religion and life philosophy card, and a variety of other life circumstances that are outside of their control. Then, throughout their lives their mission on this earth is to play the cards they've been dealt. However, as life goes along, additional cards are added to their pile. The being bullied in school card, the breakup with your high-school love card, the addiction card, the failing college card, the getting fired card, the car accident card, the children card, the getting cancer card. They feel at the mercy of these cards because each new round they are dealt causes them to feel emotions, as well as causes them to act in certain ways, in reaction to what happens to them.

They want desperately to fit in, to be accepted, to be around good people who act appropriately and who love them. They spend most of their time trying to control the world around them in attempt at meeting their own needs. They do this by arguing to get their way, changing their jobs, moving to a new location, putting out the fires, buying the item they believe will finally make them happy. But no matter where they go it seems their problems follow them. No matter what they do, in the end they're still unhappy, unfulfilled, and angry.

It feels like life is constantly throwing things at them and putting obstacles in their way. Some people react to all of these cards by working frantically to try to control them—to stop more unwanted cards from coming. Other people begin to feel helpless and that they have no hope of feeling in control of their destiny, and so they give away their power and live their lives on autopilot, simply reacting to each new card that comes. Others choose to numb themselves to the whole thing.

You can imagine that as a result, most people are pretty stressed out and unhappy. This stress leads to a variety of mental and emotional problems, such as anxiety, depression, overwhelm, hopelessness, and even guilt and shame. Most people (ourselves included) have had those experiences where we feel like we suck at life, like we're failures at being human. With the invention of social media, now we can look at everyone else's perfect Instagram photos and feel even worse about ourselves. Everyone else seems to have received a much better hand! It's not fair!

Many people have sought professional help to cope with their emotional pain and dysfunction. However, most people suffer in silence. Part of the reason most people do not seek professional help for their mental or emotional suffering is that therapists and psychiatrists have a bad reputation, partially due to the over-prescription of psychotropic medication in modern times and partially due to the horrific treatment of mental health patients in the past.

3. A BRIEF HISTORY OF CBT, REBT AND PSYCHOLOGY

Hundreds of years ago, doctors of the time were smart enough to recognize that the "mental health" problems people were having stemmed from the brain. But, they were prehistoric enough to believe that drilling holes in a person's skull or other practices that are too disturbing to mention here would solve the problem. Obviously, this did not work.

Then, around the turn of the 20th century, a new field of science immerged... psychology. Early psychologists focused on psychoanalysis, which uses talk therapy to slowly work back in time or deeper into the patient's unconscious mind, revealing and confronting root causes of their emotional problems, which stem from within the patient's past. There was also an exclusive focus on mental illness and psychological dysfunction.

Then behaviorism was the next wave of psychology, and it focused on helping people change their behaviors rather than focusing on how they felt. The person's actions were the focus, rather than their inner experience.

Both the emotional and behavioral focuses helped, but they both largely ignored the way people THINK… and it turns out they were missing the most important factor to human psychology.

To most people today, the idea that our thoughts have a significant impact on our life experience seems like common sense, even if they don't understand how it works, exactly. But, in the 1950/60s when Dr. Aaron T. Beck created CBT and Dr. Albert Ellis created REBT, they were the first to put the puzzle together that human thinking is a factor in emotional and behavioral problems. It was revolutionary!

> *"People are not disturbed by things but rather by their view of things." — Albert Ellis*

Both Beck and Ellis recognized that the process of helping a client become aware of their underlying problems and unconscious issues didn't usually lead to a change in their behavior or lives. If it did work, it took a really long time. Dr. Beck noticed that his patients who struggled with depression had what he referred to as "automatic thoughts" that were often distorted and kept them in patterns of negative emotions and behavior. Dr. Ellis recognized that patients' thoughts stemmed from beliefs were often irrational and contributed to their emotional problems and behaviors. They both began experimenting with methods of helping clients change their thoughts and beliefs in order to change their emotions and behaviors. CBT and REBT were born.

This new perspective in psychology moved toward the underlying belief that the human mind can be trained and enhanced in order to produce happiness, fulfillment, and optimum performance, and away from the focus on mental disorders and dysfunction. CBT/REBT instead, recognizes the dysfunction of the faulty programming and seeks to reprogram it. Unlike other forms of psychotherapy used then, and today, CBT/REBT focuses on the "here and now" thoughts and belief and does not go digging back into the past looking for the root of emotional problems.

When Ellis was a young man, he had a fear of talking to women. He used himself as a test subject and for a month he visited a park nearby, where he made himself talk to 100 different women. The result was that as he continued exposure to the activity that he feared, his fear diminished. This behavioral self-experiment was so successful that he began using exposure therapy, as well as a variety of other behavioral processes, as part of his therapeutic process.

Over time, it was found that much of what was previously deemed "mental illness" was, in fact, simply normal human thought dysfunction and not mental illness after all. Mental illness was no longer seen as a permanent condition or defect, but rather a result of dysfunctional, irrational thinking patterns, which could be changed. What was revolutionary about this was the realization that by changing a person's thoughts, their emotional reactions could be changed, and therefore their behaviors could be changed as well. What this meant is that for the first time psychologists believed that people could change and fix mental illness.

The reason it seems like common knowledge today is that this discovery was the biggest shift in the understanding of how the human mind works—EVER. In the 60+ years since Ellis and Beck introduced these new concepts, psychologists have learned so much more about the human mind—all thanks to the door these two opened with this new perspective. It has become clear that the original viewpoints of psychotherapy, including that the human mind was primarily dysfunctional, are not true. In fact, the human mind is resilient and adaptable. It can unlearn bad habits and create permanent, dramatic change by learning new ways of thinking. We have more control over our thoughts, emotions, and behaviors than we ever could have imagined.

By the late 1990's, the positive psychology movement that grew out of these methods was in full swing. This concept has become the focus of all of the most influential major movements in modern psychology. The self-help and human potential movement, as well as the field of life coaching, are based on this notion of self-empowerment.

Knowing this, let's look back at that hand of cards we've been dealt. While there may be specific situations that life has placed in front of us, the truth that most people do not realize is that it is not what is on the card that impacts how we feel or what we do because of it. Rather, how we PERCEIVE what we are dealt is what causes our emotional reaction. And then our emotional reaction is what determines our behavior.

This can be a really hard idea to accept for many people. Many people have become very attached to the idea that the reason they are angry is because their boss snapped at them. The reason they failed the test is because they spilled their coffee on themselves that morning, then they were late to school, and their teacher handed them a paper that they received a D on just before test time. And after all that, OF COURSE they were anxious… who wouldn't be? And, they're already a poor test taker, so under these conditions—with these cards they were dealt that day—it obviously would lead to failing the test, right?

The truth, however hard it may be to hear, is that they're wrong. None of those reasons is why they failed the test. They may have failed the test in part because they did not study and were unprepared. But, more than anything, they failed the test because they do not know how to direct their own thoughts and emotions. The truth is that they could have had a better way of thinking about each of the cards they were dealt that day. They could have chosen to ease their own anxiety. They could have been more in control of how they responded to what was happening, but they didn't know HOW because no one ever teaches this stuff!

And the person who felt angry because their boss snapped at them? Think about this… do you really think their boss reached inside of their body and created the neurotransmitters or brain chemicals that produce the feeling of anger inside of that person? No, of course not. So, where did the anger come from? It came as the body's response to an angry THOUGHT. And, while it may seem reasonable or even normal for someone to think an angry thought when someone else snaps at them, the unfortunate (or I guess fortunate) truth is that it is 100% their CHOICE what they think about it and how they allow it to make them feel. Essentially, by reacting to their boss' actions with anger, they handed their boss the right to choose *their* emotional experience. They gave away their power.

So, if at this point you're ready to swallow the pill that your thoughts and emotions and the behaviors you take because of them ARE YOUR CHOICE… read on…

Here are a couple more examples….

It wasn't your boss who handed you the "you're fired" card… you handed yourself the "getting fired" card by slacking off at work.

It wasn't the other person or God that punished you with the "getting pregnant from a 1-night stand" card… you grabbed ahold of that card all on our own by choosing to having unprotected sex with a stranger.

The most important truth that must be accepted in order to finally be in control of our own lives is the fact that WE cause most of the cards we're dealt. And the reason we choose to act in the way that brings about these things we do not want is because we act based on how we FEEL. We feel angry that we didn't get a raise and so we slack at work… and we end up getting fired. We feel desperate for attention and approval and get tipsy at the bar and it feels so good to be wanted that we let our guard down and end up with a baby with a stranger.

Our emotions drive our actions. And the key here—hear this—is that our THOUGHTS drive our emotions.

If we learn how to think differently, we can learn how to control our emotions (more of the time). And if we are in more control of our emotions, we can more deliberately choose our behaviors. And if we choose our behaviors, we can stop choosing the ones that lead to the life circumstances that we do not want.

We don't expect you to understand how this works yet or even to believe it 100%. We don't expect you to be willing to accept your own personal responsibility for your life quite yet. But, we anticipate that if you have never heard this before, you like the idea of being in control of your thoughts, emotions, and behaviors. And, if you already knew how this works to some degree, we're guessing you'd love to know HOW to do it!

4. SIMILARITIES AND DIFFERENCES BETWEEN REBT & CBT

What is CBT?

CBT stands for Cognitive Behavioral Therapy.

Cognitive refers to the process of learning and understanding through our experience, what we take in through the 5 senses, and what we think about all of it. Cognitive processes happen both consciously, meaning we are aware of them, and unconsciously, meaning they happen automatically, without our awareness.

Behavior refers to the way we act, which can happen deliberately (when we are aware of our cognitive processes) or reactively (when we are responding unconsciously to a situation).

The Core Principles of CBT

- Our thoughts create our emotions, which lead to our behaviors. We have the ability to control our thoughts, and therefore our emotions and behaviors.
- It is our perception of the situation, rather than the situation itself, that determines how we feel about it and how we react to it.
- Our perspective of a situation can change if we change the way we look at it, just like putting on a pair of glasses with a different colored lens or looking at an object from a different angle.
- When we have a negative interpretation of a situation, it causes a negative emotional reaction.
- Finding a positive viewpoint of a situation leads to improved emotional wellbeing.
- The actions we take are chosen based on what we think, and especially how we feel about a situation. Therefore, if we change the way we think, it changes our emotional state, which influences our decision making and leads to better decisions.
- When we change our negative thought process, improve our mood, and stop sabotaging behaviors, we are better able to meet our goals.

What is REBT?

REBT stands for Rational Emotive Behavioral Therapy.

Rational refers to the fact that most of the time, humans' thinking is pretty irrational. The good news is that when we think more rationally, our lives are better.

Emotive tells us that our emotions are affected by what happens, but not directly by what happens… it is our irrational thinking about what happens that causes our negative emotions.

Behavioral tells us that most of the time we act based on how we feel, and as we just said how we feel depends on what we think about what is happening around us.

The Core Principles of REBT

REBT also includes the core principles of CBT, with the following additional principles.

- You can't change the past, but you can change your beliefs about and because of the past.

- We all think irrationally, in predictable ways that are easily corrected.
- The meaning we assign a situation is both the biggest reason for our emotional reaction to it and our biggest opportunity for changing our thinking.
- Negative emotions can be both healthy and unhealthy.
- Self-acceptance is the anthesis of approval-seeking and the key to confidence.
- Releasing expectations and judgments of others is required to stop being angry and miserable.
- Accepting what is (including the parts you don't like) is the only way to take back your power.

Similarities and Differences

While CBT and REBT processes share much of their core principles, including that our behaviors and emotions are primarily caused by our attitudes, beliefs, and thoughts, there are a number of differences. The two processes focus on different aspects of cognition and have different goals. However, the two methodologies work extremely well when used together (like in this book), providing a complete process for evaluating and changing thoughts, emotions, and behaviors.

The main premise of CBT is that our thinking is distorted. This distorted thinking leads us to feel negative emotion. In order to shift the negative emotion, we need to identify the distorted thinking and shift our perspective to something more positive. By doing this, we shift our emotional reaction to the thought that we have about the situation.

The main premise of REBT is that our emotional disturbances are caused not just by the distorted thinking about a specific situation, but by irrational core beliefs.

The goal of both CBT and REBT is to change a person's emotional state and behavior, however they use different processes to achieve the desired outcome.

CBT focuses on THOUGHTS or changing the perception or interpretation of an experience. CBT is designed to help us manage our perceptions and interpretations, which can be distorted due to cognitive distortions or errors in thinking, as well as limiting beliefs. It teaches us how to become aware of and then teach us how to think more clearly, and positively. CBT helps us overcome negative, destructive thinking. But, it's not just positive thinking, it's logical, clear-minded, healthy thinking.

If you've ever made assumptions, jumped to conclusions, or made a situation worse than it was by worrying about the worst-case scenario, you have experienced a cognitive distortion.

Many of these faulty ways of thinking are obvious once you know they exist, but you don't notice them in daily life because almost all thinking happens automatically or unconsciously.

CBT also helps you tame the tormenting critical voice in your head and take your power back from others who have implanted limiting beliefs into your mind.

REBT focuses on thoughts too, but the emphasis is on changing the underlying BELIEF system that leads to the interpretation in the first place. The idea behind REBT is that by ripping the cause of the dysfunction out by the root—the core belief—it prevents the pattern of negative thinking, negative emotion, and negative behavior from continuing to happen.

Let's look at an example of how the two methodologies approach the same problem: Fear of rejection. Imagine you want to ask someone out on a second date but you're anxious about it. You tell yourself, well, she didn't smile or talk much on our first date. I don't think she's interested in me. You observed her behavior and made a judgment of what it meant but the truth is there are many other reasons that could be the cause of her behavior, other than her not being interested. CBT would call this cognitive distortion "mind reading" and would recommend you find a more positive way of looking at the situation. For example, you would identify that the assumption is just a cognitive distortion and you would then re-frame the situation by saying to yourself "I'm sure the reason she didn't smile or talk much is that she was nervous or maybe something else was going on in her life. Having a second date with her would allow us both to begin to feel comfortable with each other and get to know each other better." Changing the way you thought about it would change the way you felt about asking her on the second date, which would inspire you to be willing to reach out and ask her.

REBT would look further than the negative interpretation of the event. Instead, it would seek to identify the underlying reason you jumped to the conclusion that she wasn't interested in you. Why would your initial reaction be to assume she didn't like you? Because you're afraid of being rejected and you know that asking her out puts you at risk. What do you believe that would lead you to fear being rejected? The belief that you absolutely need her acceptance and not getting it will be awful. It will mean you're a loser who will never find a relationship that lasts." And, at an even deeper level, there would be a belief that says I need to be accepted by everyone I deem important in order to be worthy as a person." This belief is of course irrational and extreme. However, it is beliefs like this that are at the root of all of our surface level irrational thinking or cognitive distortions. It's the reason for the assumption.

So, REBT would then help identify a more rational belief to replace the irrational one. For example, simply by changing the belief to say "I really want her to accept me, but I know that not everyone is going to like me and that's okay. It does not determine the outcome I will experience with other women." By letting go of the absolute need for acceptance, the fear of rejection is softened. At this point, the likelihood of your first assumption being that she doesn't like you diminishes, and even if you do think of it, you'll quickly remind yourself that it's not the end of the world if she rejects you.

Both methods have the desired effect of helping you feel better about the situation and take action toward your goal—which is to ask her out. But, as you can see, the method of addressing the deeper level belief through REBT processes has a higher likelihood of creating long-term change.

Now that you have a general idea of the difference between the two, let's go over several distinctions that are important to understand about REBT.

Secondary Disturbance. In life, there are a variety of different things that disturb us, referred to as "disturbances" in REBT, that usually fall into two categories: a negative life experience or a negative emotional experience. It's important to note, however, that sometimes a life experience is not actually negative, however the person's interpretation of it makes it negative and causes a negative emotional reaction to it. CBT would look at this and say that the life experience simply is what it is, while the negative emotional experience is usually caused by the way that we think about the life experiences. REBT would acknowledge another layer of disturbance that happens when not only do you feel anxious because you are going to ask the woman on a date, you are afraid of feeling anxious while asking her or while on the date. You're anxious about being anxious. You're worrying about worrying. This is a secondary disturbance. Disturbing yourself about your emotional disturbance that you have about the actual, original life disturbance is too much for anyone to handle, which is why these secondary disturbances are often the major factor in severe depression, anxiety, and panic.

Another common secondary disturbance is guilt. Say you have anger problems and tend to snap at people you love. You then feel guilty for not controlling your rage. Another great example is someone who is working on overcoming his or her problems and feels like they're not making progress as fast as they think they "should" be able to. They have their problem and the stress it causes, plus the additional layer of emotional disturbance due to beating themselves up about it.

Often, in order to deal with the primary problem, the secondary disturbance must be addressed first. For instance, if a person cannot stop judging themselves for their nervous behavior, it makes it a lot harder for them to address the underlying problem because every time they're asked to reflect on their experience of anxiety, they feel anxious about it, which clouds their thinking.

Unconditional Self-Acceptance. CBT often focuses on improving a person's self-esteem by reinforcing their positive qualities and affirm their worthiness. When we teach about confidence (we have a whole book and course on it) we take it a step further. The truth is that trying to feel good about yourself by thinking you're good at something actually works against because if you need to believe you are good at something to feel good about yourself, failure or trying a new skills you're not good at yet will lower your self-esteem. True confidence is the belief that you are always able to learn and improve in any area, which is called having a growth mindset, which we'll talk about next.

REBT has a different method for improving self-esteem, which is unconditional self-acceptance. It encourages people to stop self-rating and instead accept themselves as imperfect human beings, regardless of their traits or behaviors or how others see them. Instead of rating their SELF, they would evaluate the results of their actions and behaviors and seek to change them, not because of a negative judgment of those behaviors but because of the undesirable outcomes because of them.

Later in this course, we'll get into more detail about unconditional acceptance.

Helpful Negative Emotions. Unlike CBT and most other cognitive therapies, REBT differentiates between self-destructive, inappropriate negative emotions and helpful, appropriate negative emotions. Anxiety, depression, and anger are examples considered unhealthy negative emotions, while sadness, sorrow, concern, or regret are considered healthy emotions. Later in this course we'll get into more detail about healthy and unhealthy emotions.

For example, if you feel intense sadness and grief when you lose a loved one, this is completely appropriate and healthy. However, if you feel anxious about arriving late to a meeting, this is unhealthy because the reason behind your anxiety is the fear of judgment and rigid thinking that says you must never be late to a meeting. While you may believe it seems reasonable to feel anxious if you're going to be late, the truth is that feeling anxious does not help the situation or make you get there faster. All it does is make your ride unpleasant and put you in a negative emotional state when entering the meeting. There is also a difference between moderate anxiety in that situation vs. panicking about it. The power of REBT and CBT is that they give you tools that help you learn how to manage these emotional reactions, making whether you feel anxious when you're late to a meeting or not a *choice*.

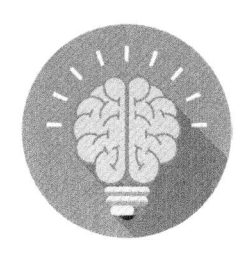

SECTION 2: THE GROWTH MINDSET

1: WHY THE GROWTH MINDSET IS THE KEY TO CHANGING YOUR MIND

There is one core underlying belief that needs to be developed in order for CBT and REBT to be effective: The Growth Mindset which basically means believing that you CAN change your thoughts and behaviors.

If you don't believe you can change, you won't.

Two Key Underlying Psychological Principles:

1) Locus of control: what you believe is and is not within your control. Some people feel like life is simply happening to them, like they're a victim to whatever might happen. They have an external locus of control.

Other people believe they are in control of their lives. Even when something happens to them that appears to come from the outside, they still see how they have power over the outcome. This is an internal locus of control.

How do you develop an internal locus of control and feel empowered about your life?

2) Develop a bias toward action. If you feel like your life is out of your control, you're unlikely to take action because you don't believe it will make a difference. You have a bias toward inaction. So, in order to overcome this, you can begin taking action and seeing what happens. Doing this over time shows yourself that you have more influence over your life than you thought. You develop a bias toward action, meaning you

believe you're the type of person who takes action to influence their own life. This, in turn, develops your internal locus of control and makes you feel empowered to direct your own life. It gives you confidence.

But, there is one core underlying psychological principle that is even more important to understand: the Growth Mindset.

People who have this mindset are:
- More resilient
- Better at coping with failure
- More likely to challenge themselves
- Those who do not have it are:
- Less resilient
- Poor at coping with failure
- Avoid challenges that could reveal their flaws

QUIZ:

Consider this example and how you would feel if it was you. Imagine that you had a terrible day. You spilled coffee on your shirt on the way to work, you got a parking ticket on your lunch break, and your boss reprimanded you for publishing a document with several major errors. How would you react?

a) You'd feel bad about yourself for being clumsy, unintelligent and unlucky. You'd accept that this is just how your life goes.
b) You'd be upset but you'd be thinking about how you should probably use a better travel mug, be more careful when you park, and double check your work.

Then, I want you to answer these questions:
- If I told you that your intelligence, like an IQ score, is something about you that you can't change, would you:
  a) agree
  b) disagree
- If I told you that talents are something you are born with would you:
  a) agree
  b) disagree

So, did you answer mostly a's or b's?

Before you dive into what this all means, the number 1 most important thing you need to know about it is: If you don't already have this mindset, you can LEARN IT.

This core belief system is called the Growth Mindset. And the opposite way of viewing the world is called the Fixed Mindset.

If you answered all b's, you have a growth mindset. If you answered some a's, that's okay, because your answers to those questions will be very different by the time you finish this book!

Growth Mindset

The growth mindset is a belief that your basic qualities, including intelligence and talent, can be cultivated through effort. This means that while people may be innately different, with certain aptitudes and temperaments, all aspects of a person's abilities and personality can be changed, regardless of where your setpoint is.

Fixed Mindset

The fixed mindset, on the other hand, is a belief that these same characteristics are fixed at birth or become locked-in by a certain age. This means that some people are just inherently more talented or intelligent than others and that's just the way it is.

If you feel like at least part of you believes that intelligence and talent are fixed, you are not alone. Most people, especially in the western world, believe this because our culture teaches us that it's true. So, it's not your fault. Emphasis is put on testing us to determine our intelligence, such as taking an IQ test or being graded. No one stops to think that a single test taken on a certain day at a certain age cannot possibly predict how well you would do on the test years later, after learning more, or when you're in a better mood. But, we're taught that these tests identify what we've got and that's it. We're stuck with it.

We also live in a culture that is obsessed with "natural talent". There are 2 problems with this.
1. The people who work hard to develop their abilities far out-win the naturals in the long run.
2. If being a natural is so important, it actually discourages the effort it takes for those who have to work at it.

And, that's exactly what happens.

People with a fixed mindset believe they'll always have the same level of talent regardless of how much effort they put in. They've either got it or they don't. Because of this the spend a lot of effort trying to prove their abilities and intelligence. They want to look smart. So, if they're not immediately good at something, they stop doing it. This is because they're in a constant quest to prove that they are talented or intelligent. To a fixed mindset person, effort is a bad thing. Having to work hard at something is a signal that you're not a natural talent or that you're not of high intelligent because if you were you wouldn't' have to try. As a result, they don't challenge themselves, they don't like trying new things, and so they never develop their potential. They're trapped reaching only as far as their current abilities can take them. They're trapped because failure is devastating. It means they are a failure. And because they don't want to have to take on an identity as a failure, they'll often blame others or the outside world. Fixed mindset people find joy in being the best or being judged as talented or smart.

Growth mindset people see the world very differently. They believe that the more effort they put into something, whether it's practicing or learning, the better they will become. If they're not good at something they see it as a sign that they have to work harder. They have little need to prove they are talented or intelligent and instead are on a never-ending quest to continue to grow. How hard someone tries is how they measure the person's value. They enjoy challenges and see them as an opportunity to learn something and expand their boundaries. They may not like failing, but they don't ever believe they are a failure. They see failure as a learning experience. Growth mindset people find joy in progress and learning.

So, what is important to know here is that if you didn't already know that you can change and improve your talents, skills, intelligence, characteristics, and behaviors, now you know! It's also important to keep in mind that no one is either 100% fixed or 100% growth oriented. Everyone is on a spectrum. Plus, you can think fixed in one area, such as believing your intelligence is fixed, while believe you can grow in another area, such as your singing ability.

And remember, this is important because the rest of this program will be helping you change the way you think so that you can change the way you behave, which will change your experience of life in any area that desire. Understanding the growth mindset matters because if you want to develop your confidence you have to believe that your level of confidence is not limited by a fixed personality trait. If you want to learn how to speak in public, you have to believe that your fear and timidity are not in-born characteristics that you're stuck with. If you want to explore a new career that challenges you to learn skills and knowledge that you've struggled with in the past, like math for instance, you have to believe you're capable of learning and that your intelligence in that area is not fixed.

2: LOCUS OF CONTROL

When we try to create a new story, one of the most important things is to focus on the things that we can control. Too often we waste time and energy on things that are outside of our control and influence, when we could be spending it on creating our new story. In fact, this is why many people never create their new story—they are focused on changing the wrong things. We need to direct our focus on things we CAN control—things within our "circle of control".

There are 3 levels of influence:
1. Things that you can directly control
2. Things you can influence
3. Things that you have no control and influence.

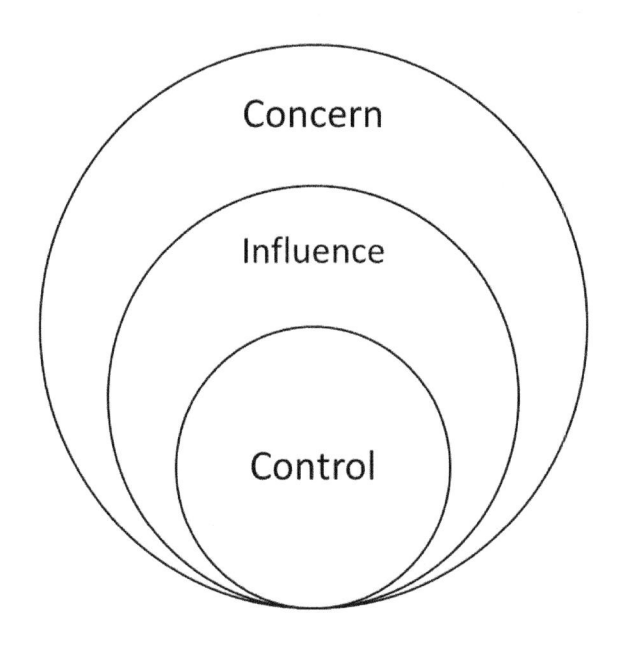

Things you CAN control:

It's important to recognize that our perception of what we can control strongly influences what we do and what we feel about situations in our life. The perception of how much control you have in your life is called "Locus of Control."

A person who has a predominant internal locus of control believes that they can (or should be able to) influence all of the events and outcomes in their life. On the other hand, someone who has a predominantly external locus of control tends to blame the outside world for nearly all things that happen in their life. As you can probably see, being at the extreme end of both of these tendencies can have a negative impact on your life. For example, someone with a high internal locus of control tends to blame himself or herself, and beat themselves up, when something does not go their way, even if they had no control of the outcome. In other words, it is important to recognize that there are things we do not have control over. On the other hand, someone with a high external locus of control tends not to take responsibility for anything, blaming everyone else for things that are clearly within their control. They don't take control of their life because they do not think that they have the power to make the difference. People with a balanced locus of control have a realistic view of what they do have power over.

Below is a small list of things that you do have control over right now:
- How much effort you put into something
- How many times you smile, say "thank you", or show appreciation today
- How well you prepare for something
- How you react to an emotion (yes, you have a choice—in fact, we made a whole book about it)
- What you focus on
- How you interpret a situation
- What you commit to doing or not doing
- What conversations you have and what you engage in
- How much you focus on the present moment
- What you tell yourself and how nice you are to YOU
- How you take care of your body
- How many new things you are exposed to

- What you do in your free time
- Whom you spend your time with and who your friends are
- What information you consume: books you read, media you listen to or watch
- When you ask for help
- Whether you make plans and act on them
- How much you believe what other people say
- How long it takes you to try again when you fail

This is just a small list of examples. However, notice that all of these items are DIRECTLY related to YOU. Yes, YOU, your actions, thoughts, emotions, beliefs and choices are what are within your circle of control.

Remember that some of the things that you have control over have consequences, but those consequences do not take away from the fact that you have a choice.

- What are things that do you have control over that you would want to change and take charge of?

- How will taking control help you create your new story?

Things you CAN influence:

Outside of your circle of control, the next level is your sphere of influence. Our influence and perceived influence is critical to our wellbeing. In fact, researchers, Dr. Sommer and Dr. Bourgeois have been able to show that the more influential you feel you are, the greater your happiness and wellbeing. This is because feeling that we influence others gives us a sense of purpose, meaning, and control. Notice that influence is different than control. Influence does not mean telling people what to do or making them do something. That does not lead to happiness. And, the truth is that you CAN'T make people do anything.

There are two ways that you can increase your level of happiness when it comes to our influence.
- Increase your influence on others around you. The type of influence we're talking about here is being a leader in our inner cir-

cle—meaning leading by example. For example, when we follow our dreams, stand up for what we believe, and when we grow, we empower other around us to do the same thing. It is about living in the reality that if you change your behavior, or attitude, other people tend to notice and are affected by those changes whether they want to or not.

- Increasing your awareness of how you currently influence those around you. When you acknowledge the positive impact you are having on others, it boosts your confidence.

Influence is a normal part of human nature. It's up to you to decide in what ways you are influenced by others and whether you are a good influence on those around you. The sphere of influence goes both ways because the people that you may have influence over also influence you. Choose who you are around wisely, and be aware of the impact you have on others.

Make a list of those closest to you whom you influence and/or who influence you:

- How do you influence them (both negative and positively)?

- How can you become a better positive influence on them?

- How do they influence you (both positive and negative)?

- Are there any negative influencers that you can replace with positive ones?

Becoming a positive influencer will increase your happiness and wellbeing. Living your new story will serve as an empowering example for others. But, keep an eye out for the negative influencers in your life that may hinder the story that you are trying to create.

3: DEVELOPING A GROWTH MINDSET STEP 1: AWARENESS

Now that you know what a growth mindset is and why it is such an important belief system, you can begin to practice this way of thinking.

Awareness of Your Self-Talk and Fixed Mindset Triggers

Everyone has an internal voice, and part of this voice is an inner critic, inner hater, or inner doubter—it is the fixed mindset persona. You can hear this persona within the negative self-talk that happens in your thoughts and mind. It can sound like:

- I'm not good enough.
- I will probably fail.
- I can't do this.
- I don't want to risk it.
- I shouldn't have to try so hard.
- If I'm not naturally good at this, I should just quit.
- It's not my fault.
- This makes me uncomfortable, I'm not doing it.
- Why try if it won't change anything?

What does yours often sound like?

Give Your Fixed Mindset Persona a Name

Naming it helps you remind yourself that this mindset—or habit of thinking—is not who you are!

I will call my fixed mindset persona: _____

Identify Your Triggers

What situations tend to trigger your fixed mindset persona?
- When you're thinking about taking on a big challenge or learning something new?

    ___always   ___ sometimes   ___never

What does your fixed mindset persona tell you when you're in this situation?

- When you're thinking about making a change?
    ___always   ___ sometimes   ___never

    What does your fixed mindset persona tell you when you're in this situation?

- When someone criticizes you?
    ___always   ___ sometimes   ___never

    What does your fixed mindset persona tell you when you're in this situation?

- When you fail at something?
    ___always   ___ sometimes   ___never

    What does your fixed mindset persona tell you when you're in this situation?

- When something goes wrong? Do you beat yourself up or blame someone else?
    ___always   ___ sometimes   ___never

    What does your fixed mindset persona tell you when you're in this situation?

- When someone else makes a mistake? Do you judge them? Criticize them?
    ___always   ___ sometimes   ___never

What does your fixed mindset persona tell you when you're in this situation?

- When you're under pressure or on a deadline?
  ___always   ___ sometimes   ___never

  What does your fixed mindset persona tell you when you're in this situation?

- When you procrastinate or are feeling lazy?
  ___always   ___ sometimes   ___never

  What does your fixed mindset persona tell you when you're in this situation?

- When you have a conflict with someone?
  ___always   ___ sometimes   ___never

  What does your fixed mindset persona tell you when you're in this situation?

- When your reputation is at risk or you worry what others will think?
  ___always   ___ sometimes   ___never

  What does your fixed mindset persona tell you when you're in this situation?

Awareness of Your Reaction
- Ask yourself, how am I rationalizing or judging the situation?

- How am I beating myself up or blaming others?

- What is the fixed mindset telling me?

4: DEVELOPING A GROWTH MINDSET STEP 2: PERSPECTIVE

You may not always be able to change what happens around you, but you always have a choice of how you respond, react, and how you view the situation. When you catch your fixed mindset persona with a limited thought, ask yourself:

- What else might be going on here?
- What is a more realistic and optimistic way to look at this situation?
- What are the good aspects of this situation?
- How can I look at this differently?

Here are examples of rephrasing fixed mindset thinking as growth mindset thinking. Be on the lookout for any time you hear your fixed mindset persona taking over your internal dialogue, such as the reactions to the triggers you identified or the following common fixed mindset thoughts, you can change your perspective to a growth mindset,

- When you hear yourself thinking something like: "What if you're not good enough? You'll be a failure."
- Change it to: "Everyone starts out not being good and successful people all fail along the way."
- When you hear yourself thinking: "If it's this hard, you're probably just not good at it."

- Change it to: "If it's hard, it means I need to put in more effort and it will be a great achievement when I get good at it."
- When you hear yourself thinking: "If I don't try, I can't fail and I will keep my dignity."
- Change it to: "If I don't try, I have already failed and I have no dignity."
- When you hear yourself thinking: "It's not my fault."
- Change it to: "If I don't accept whatever part of this is my responsibility, I give away my power."

Go back through the fixed mindset triggers you identified and what your persona tends to tell you and rewrite a NEW thought from the growth mindset perspective.

- My fixed mindset trigger thought:

- My replacement growth mindset perspective:

- My fixed mindset trigger thought:

- My replacement growth mindset perspective:

- My fixed mindset trigger thought:

- My replacement growth mindset perspective:

- My fixed mindset trigger thought:

- My replacement growth mindset perspective:

5: DEVELOPING A GROWTH MINDSET
STEP 3: ACTION

So, at this point you've noticed your fixed mindset persona thinking limited thoughts and you've changed your perspective. The next step is the most important, and in fact is what truly makes someone have a growth mindset. The most important factor for developing a growth mindset is action.

- As yourself, what did you learn from the experience?

- What could you do differently next time or going forward?

- What would help you achieve this goal that you haven't tried?

- What do you need to learn or what information do you need to gather?

- What steps will you take?

DON'T STOP THERE!

List out the steps that you will take, and for each one, identify exactly WHEN you will do it. If anything on your list cannot happen within 1 week, save it for later and re-assess at the end of the week. For everything else, include when you will do it and what you need in order to do it.

Lastly, take 5 minutes to visualize yourself taking each of these steps, as you imagine they will play out, including achieving the goal and outcome you are aiming for.

Practicing a Growth Mindset

Select your favorite affirmations from the list below or write your own and put them somewhere you will see them every day, such as next to your bed, on your mirror, on the cover of your day planner, attached to your computer screen, or programmed into the calendar of your phone to remind you to look at them every day, at least once.

The Growth Mindset

- Everyone has a fixed mindset to some degree. Now that I know the difference and I know I can change, I am developing a growth mindset.
- Challenges, risks, and failures do not reflect that I am a failure, they are opportunities for me to grow and improve.
- I care more about the process and the journey and who I become along the way than I do about the outcome.
- I am glad that I am not perfect and that I never will be because it means I am not limited to where I am today.
- What other people think about me is none of my business. I no longer allow other people's opinions and judgments to hold me back from living a life of fulfillment and reaching my potential.
- I am always looking for the meaning and lessons contained in all situations that can help me fulfill the greater purpose in my life.
- I move past the discomfort of making mistakes quickly because I learn the lesson and allow it to help me improve so I can do better next time.
- I know that no one starts out great at something and so I am willing to try new things and practice skills I would like to have, putting in the time and effort I know it takes to master this area.
- I am the master of my thoughts, emotions, and actions and I do not give my power away by reacting to others criticism, judgment, or actions in a negative way.
- Having to exert effort in order to be good at something is a good thing because it shows me that I am capable of learning and improving. I love knowing I am not limited to my current strengths.
- I love knowing that even if someone else may be more naturally talented in an area than I am, a person with better work ethic will out-perform a person with talent every time.
- I know that most truly successful people have failed their way to success.
- I have skills and knowledge today that I didn't have before because I learned and grew in those areas, so I know I can develop any ability I want.
- If my talents, abilities, and intelligence are not fixed, this means my potential is truly limitless!

- Write your own:

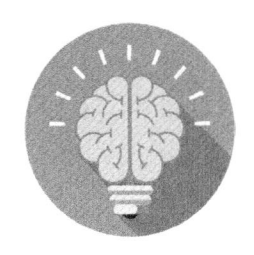

SECTION 3: HOW THE MIND WORKS

1: THOUGHTS CREATE EMOTIONS AND BEHAVIORS

As we've established, CBT is based on the premise that our thoughts create our emotions and influence our behavior. The 3 aspects—thoughts, emotions, behaviors—interplay and influence each other, however the area where we have the most power is our thoughts because they are almost always the foundation of our emotions and the behaviors that we take because of them. The good news, which is why CBT is so powerful, is that because we can learn to have greater control over our thoughts, we can have greater control over our emotions and our behaviors.

As discussed in the "What is CBT" chapter, cognition includes the processes of thinking as well as processing an experience, including what is taken in by the 5 senses. When you experience anything in life, it is interpreted by your brain, which means in a split second your brain compares what it is taking in through your senses, which tells it what is going on in your experience, to everything else you've ever experienced. It's trying to make a snap judgment of:

- What is going on
- What it means
- How you should feel about it
- What you should do

The brain has evolved to rapidly interpret everything you experience and it's so good at it that you don't even notice it's happening. That is, until something happens that causes your mind to interpret a situation as negative. It chooses a perspective or belief about the situation that creates an emotional reaction in your body. It's unpleasant, so it's noticeable. Your body reacts to this emotion, which is actually caused by the thought triggering your body to release any of a number of brain chemicals, often referred to as neurotransmitters or endorphins or hormones. Your brain is like a chemical factory and there is a different neurotransmitter that is responsible for every emotion you can feel.

It all functions as it should. Something threatens you, your brain interprets, triggers the hormones that shoot throughout your body inspiring you spring into action. Someone tells you they adore you and you're flooded with feel-good chemicals. Our bodies and brain are amazing machines. But sometimes, these emotional reactions get out of whack with what's actually happening. You can feel anxious for no reason. Something small makes you furious. You're sad even when you're doing something that usually makes you happy.

What's happened is that your mind has learned a pattern of thinking that is faulty. Your brain is interpreting situations negatively, when they're not. Your mind is judging situations, or yourself. You have unconscious limiting beliefs impacting your perspective that you aren't aware of. Your brain was doing what it does best—trying to interpret your world in a way that protects you. Unfortunately, as you lived life, your brain got programmed by the world around you. Your thoughts were influenced by the actions of others. Your core beliefs were adopted from the beliefs of others. And because you weren't aware of any of this, your mind became trapped by its own faulty beliefs. Your thoughts run amok and you were never taught how to catch them.

It happens to everyone. Humans bodies and brains don't come with an owners' manual! But the good news is that the solution is simple. You can become more aware of this process. You can change your thought patterns and beliefs. You can reprogram yourself. You can become conscious of your unconscious thoughts and behaviors. You can choose to experience more positive emotions, and less negative ones.

You have this power to control your own mind—a power that has been withheld from you your entire life. And it's time to take your power back!

Let's Look at Emotions

The best place to start a discussion about how thinking works and impacts your life is to look at emotions. Let me ask you a question, should emotions be trusted?

Some people say, "You should always trust your emotions."

Other people say, "Feelings are irrational and can't be trusted."

So, which is it?

They're BOTH wrong.

Emotions and feelings are neither right nor wrong, accurate or not. Emotions are simply your body's reaction to what you are THINKING. Your belief system and other unconscious thoughts are happening on autopilot all the time, and cause emotions. That's why sometimes you have NO IDEA why you feel the way you do.

So, here's an example of why emotions are never either right or wrong... because they're just reacting to your thoughts...

Think about something that you really, really wish you had, but that you don't have. I wish I had:

You may feel unhappy because you don't have it, but that's not true. You are unhappy because of the THOUGHT of not having it.

Let me prove it to you:

Have you ever been happy while not having this thing you want?

__Yes __No

If you didn't have it but you didn't care that you didn't have it, could you be unhappy?

__Yes __No

If you didn't have it but were doing something else that kept you from thinking about it, such as going down a roller coaster, would you be unhappy about it? No.

You see, not having what you want doesn't make you feel bad.

Thinking about it does.

Where Do Emotions Come From?

Sometimes our unconscious mind and senses are picking up cues from our environment that trigger emotions, such as reading a person's body language or facial expression and having an automatic physiological response or sensing danger and having an automatic fear response. *(By the way, to learn more about the fight-or-flight response that causes you to feel fear and anxiety, check out the Situational vs Psychological Fear chapter in the Developing Awareness section.)*

However, most of the time it is NOT the outside world or the situation that is happening that causes our emotional reaction—it's what we're thinking. It is the mental filter that the situation passes through—aka, our interpretation—that then causes our emotional reaction to the situation.

Situation (activating event) → Inference (automatic thought) → Emotion

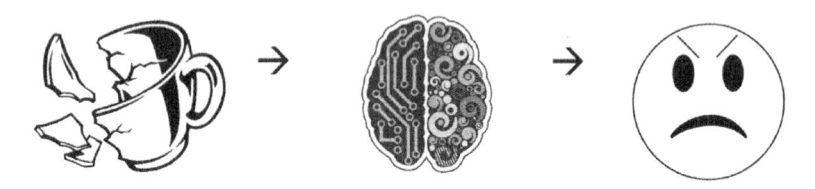

The key to understand here is that research over decades on CBT provides evidence that we can have control over our thoughts. And if we have control over our thoughts, we can control our emotions. It may be challenging to do this, but it is a skill that can be learned. Here's the process:

Recognize Emotion → Identify Thought → Change Thought → Change Emotion

Changing the Thought

Once you notice that a thought is happening it becomes conscious. Since you're aware of it, you can then choose to change it. Your mind automatically interpreted the situation, but now that you're paying attention to it you can choose a different interpretation—a different perspective. This is great news because when you change the way you look at things, the things you look at change. Even in the same situation or with the same facts, if you change your viewpoint, your experience of the situation will change. Here is an example: a man was visiting a friend's house and went into the kitchen to make some tea. He didn't find a tea kettle, and so poured water into a glass coffee carafe and placed it on the gas stove. He returned to the living room and minute later smelled something burning. He returned and found that the handle of the carafe had caught fire. He quickly put the fire out. He apologized to his friend and was feeling both embarrassed and guilty. His friend, however, was laughing and complemented him on his "fireman" skills. Same situation, different perspectives—and the result was completely different emotional responses.

Why this matters!

So, this matters because, of course, you want to feel better. If you change your perspective of a situation, you will change your emotional reaction to it. But, it's even better than that!

You see, your emotions are the driving force for your BEHAVIORS because the decisions you make are based on how you feel. As you get better at being aware of your emotions and thinking, you'll be able to make decisions from a place of control—you might feel a certain way, but you'll use your cognitive processes to choose to act from a place of rational thought.

But, if you're like most people, you're not at that place yet—at least not all the time.

So, here's where we are now:

Thought → Emotion → Decisions → Action

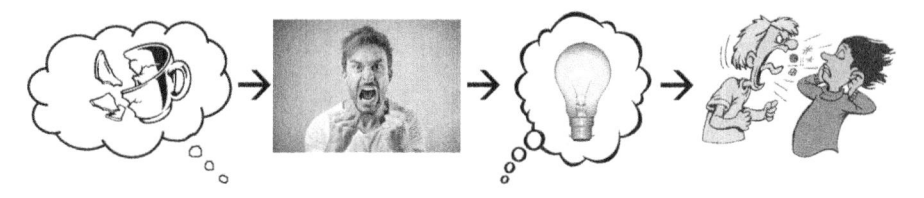

The behaviors you exhibit and the actions you take are a direct result of your thoughts. So, if you are experiencing behaviors you don't like or have been doing things you aren't pleased with, your thoughts are to blame.

If you can't yet see the behaviors or actions you're doing that aren't serving you, look around at your life at the results you're experiencing. Have you been having any problems at work or in your relationships? Have you experienced anything unpleasant? Are there are things you want that you don't have? On the positive side, what aspects of your life have you managed to create that you want, enjoy, or love?

The reason I ask is because I'm going to take this cause and effect train one more step.

Thought → Emotion → Decisions → Action → Results

That's right, your behaviors and actions are what determine the results and outcomes you experience in your life—both the wanted ones and the unwanted ones.

By changing your thoughts, you can literally transform your life. Literally! So, let's dive into more about understanding how thinking works.

2: WE ALL THINK IRRATIONALLY! YES, EVEN YOU!

It's really easy to notice when someone else is thinking irrationally. What they say sounds illogical. It makes no sense! Even if you try to point out their error in thinking, they don't get it. They seem locked into their point of view, like they're blinded to the truth. It can be frustrating. But, the truth is that the same thing happens to you.

Sometimes we all become blind to logic. Why? Because of the way our minds work.

You brain's number 1 goal at all times is to keep you safe, and so it focuses on evaluating what is happening right now and predicting what is going to happen in the future. And while it is interpreting your world, it is very easy to misperceive or misunderstand situations that are happening around you or things people say to you. There are a variety of reasons for this.

First, at all times you are receiving limited information. One reason this happens is that literally we may just not know all of the facts. If you hear a loud bang outside, you cannot see what is happening and so may assume it's a gunshot when it's simply a car door. Your friend may sound irritated, and so you assume they're mad at you, but the truth is that you don't know what happened to them earlier in the day that may have them upset.

The other reason you are receiving limited information is because your brain is blocking out most of the information happening around you. The reason for this is because there are millions of bits of information going on around you all the time that could be picked up by your senses, however if you were consciously aware of it all you would go crazy. For this reason, your brain has a focusing mechanism called the Reticular Activating System that narrows down those millions of bits into 2,000 that are relevant to you. So, depending on whatever you're focusing on at the time, your brain picks up on data relevant to that topic. If you're at the airport and you've been talking to your sister about her baby, you notice all the babies crying as you walk through the terminal. If you are dressed in a suit and heading to an important meeting, you'll notice all of the other people dressed up who look like they're up to something important too. But, your brain literally blocks out almost everything.

Next, whatever information your brain does have access to gets filtered through what is already in your brain. For instance, your brain takes this input and compares it to your beliefs to determine what you think about this information. It also searches through your memories to see what has happened in your past that in any way relates to this information, so it knows what it is. For instance, when a baby sees a four legged creature that's hairy and his parent calls it a dog, the next time the baby sees a four legged hairy creature he calls it "dog". But this time it's a cat. He does not know this because the only belief he had was that four legged hairy things are called dogs. Now, imagine the baby had been bit by a dog. Now, the next time it sees a four legged creature the baby's brain is going to quickly evaluate this creature against the baby's belief systems and memories of past experiences, which of course will lead the baby to conclude this creature is a dog and dogs are something to be afraid of. The baby reacts to the dog with fear. The problem is that it's not a dog—it's an adorable bunny. The baby's thinking is irrational.

But the truth is, it is not that the baby is irrational—because based on what he knows it's actually quite smart to fear the bunny. This same exact processes is happening to all adults too, all of the time, in a split second. Irrational thinking happens because we have limited information about what is happening and we interpret it through our biased beliefs and memories of our experience, which are limited, not to mention memories are very often not accurate.

It's important to recognize that thinking irrationally does not mean we're doing anything wrong—just like the example with the baby, the truth is that our irrational thoughts actually DO MAKE SENSE based on our limited understanding.

The problem with irrational thinking is when it becomes problematic and negatively impacts our lives.

So, when we talk about irrational thinking, we are specifically referring to situations where this thinking:

1. Limits or blocks a person from being able to function in life and achieve their goals.
2. Causes extreme emotional reactions that lead a person to behaviors that harm themselves, others, or their opportunities in life.
3. Distorts reality, meaning that the thoughts are ignoring reality or facts in a way that is hindering a person's ability to make rational decisions or understand what is happening, in a way that has negative consequences.
4. Causes the person to judge and evaluate other people, themselves, or the world in a way that is harmful

As you can see, irrational thoughts are self-defeating and negatively impact our lives. If we do not learn how to identify and challenge our irrational thinking, we will continue to judge ourselves and others, remain blind to truths that could change our lives, experience emotional disturbances that harm us, and hold ourselves back from living our potential.

3: COGNITIVE DISTORTIONS

CBT techniques are designed to help people overcome their faulty programming. You see, we all have common ways that our thought processes are dysfunctional, called cognitive distortions. These inaccurate thoughts reinforce negative thinking patterns and emotions and convince us of a reality that is simply not true. It can be liberating just hearing about these distortions because once you recognize that the reality you assume isn't necessarily 100% accurate, you can open up to greater possibilities! Even people who pride themselves on being critical thinkers can get stuck in these traps. We'll go over them in this chapter and then techniques and activities we explore in the rest of the book will provide methods for overcoming these limitations.

All-or-Nothing / Polarized Thinking

This distortion is also known as "Black-and-White Thinking," and it occurs when a person is not able to see the gray areas of any situations. In other words, the person may not be able to or willing to see that there may be other factors or different options in any situation. Therefore, they stay stuck between two extremes which makes them hard to compromise with others or make a decision. For example, everything is either perfect or awful there is not room for all the emotions and experiences that can be in between. Another example may be a person that fails in something may think that they are a total failure without recognizing that they may need to improve in an area in their life and that the single failure does not define them and their capabilities.

Overgeneralization

In this distortion a person overgeneralizes things in their life, such as defining a single occurrence as an overall pattern. For example, a person may have a misunderstanding while communicating with a friend and then assume that they are just bad at communicating with everyone. They may even generalize further and believe they are disliked by everyone. Therefore, this bias leads to negative thoughts about the person's life in general, based on one or two experiences that they feel defines them. In others words, a single incident is used as evidence to conclude something. The biggest challenge with overgeneralizing is that we may define our abilities or characteristics based one experience and then stop trying in future situations because if that one experience.

Jumping to Conclusions

(This can look like making assumptions or mind reading.) This distortion happens when we assume what the other person is thinking, or what their intentions are. It is true that at times we may have a general idea of why a person may do something, but we usually don't acknowledge that our assumptions may be erroneous. Therefore, we may see someone and their nonverbal reaction and assume that they may not be interested in what we have to say when they may actually simply be distracted with something else in their life. We may even think that they are thinking something negative about us when that the truth may be far from that reality. Our predictions and conclusions are typically based on our own biases instead of reality. We may even conclude that our fear may come true and avoid a situation before we have a chance to find out.

Magnification (Catastrophizing) or Minimization

This distortion is when you exaggerate the meaning of something, or on the other extreme you minimize it. For example, a person may make a mistake at work and may magnify that mistake to make it seem like they will ruin the project that the company is working on. At the same time a person may get an award for something and minimize it and still believe that they are still not good enough. This leads people to always look at worst case scenarios.

Emotional Reasoning

This is an important distortion that people must identify and address because it's common. Emotional reasoning is when we take our emotions as a fact. In other words, if we feel it then it must be true, and we find reasons to justify it. For example, if we feel dumb or unattractive in our current moment then we believe it must be an overall fact of who we are. We feel that way, therefore it's real. However, the truth is that our emotional state in a given moment on a specific topic is rarely indicative of reality. Unfortunately, for many it is difficult to see past their current emotional state.

Should Statements

Another common distortion is "should" statements. You may have noticed times when you are telling yourself that you should do this, should not do that, or must do this other thing. The truth about should statements is that they are almost always based on what we think others around us believe we should do, rather than what we truly want. The problem is we often create "shoulds" and expectations for ourselves that are unrealistic and hard to meet and then beat up ourselves and feel guilty because of them. And worse, we don't even actually believe them and we're doing it for everyone else. This leads to us making decisions that don't benefit us short term or long term. At the same time, we also place shoulds and expectations on others and when they do not meet our requirements it may lead to anger and resentment. (We talk about should more in the Awareness of Self-Talk, Part 2 chapter.)

Labeling and Mislabeling

This is another form of overgeneralizing—a tendency to assign a judgment or label based on a single event or instance. We allow the event to define ourselves or others. If you're golfing and you miss your put and lose, you tell yourself "I'm a loser" instead of simply "I goofed this one up." This happened, and therefore I am that. You can also label others. For instance, if you meet someone that does not say hello right away you may label them as a mean person who does not like you, when in reality the person may have been distracted and it had nothing to do with you. Not only did you assume the person's intentions, you judged and labeled them. With labeling, you're overgeneralizing a single trait as the main definition of yourself or others. Mislabeling is when you apply a label that is not just overgeneralized, it is inaccurate and usually uses highly emotional and exaggerated language. For example, calling yourself or someone else a pig.

Personalization

This distortion is also a common one that many people can relate to and have experience at some point of their life. It involves us taking things personally and blaming ourselves for something in an illogical way. For instance, you may believe someone is acting a certain way because of you when it has nothing to do with you. In extreme cases you may assume that you are the cause of the moods or behaviors of those around us. When bad things happen around you, you think it's your fault. For example, if you are late to a meeting and then the meeting is a disaster, you may tell yourself that everything would have been fine if you were early, when the reality is that the outcome had nothing to do with you.

Blaming

On the other end of the spectrum from people who personalize everything, there are the people that never take responsibilities for their action. This fallacy of blaming leads us to blame others for what goes wrong, and not just the outcomes—we even blame others for our emotions, thoughts, and behavior without realizing that we can always choose our emotions and behaviors.

Fallacy of Fairness

This is another common fallacy. We would all like to believe that life is fair however, reality is that life can be unfair at times. Unfairness can cause negative emotions. Some people may find themselves judging a situation based on whether something is fair or not, rather than looking at the objective reality, which will only lead to anger, resentment, and hopelessness. Therefore, it's important to come to acceptance that some things will go our way and some things won't and that we can always choose to make the best of any situation instead of judging it, which adds another layer of stress or anger. Another aspect of this is the "just world hypothesis" which is the belief that the world is just and, therefore, if something bad happens to someone it has to be because they deserved it. This can lead people to judge, reject, and blame others because of the bad things that happen to that person—even if it is clearly not their fault. People also judge, reject, and blame themselves, and when bad things happen to them, they believe it means they are bad.

Fallacy of Change

This is the belief and expectation that we can change others to meet our needs. A person experiencing this may put pressure on others and attempt to force them to meet his or her needs. Not only do they believe others can or will change and bend to their will, which they won't, the main issue is the belief that their own success and happiness depends on other people being what they want them to be and meeting their needs. This leads to a lack of taking personal responsibility for meeting their own needs and causes resentment for both parties when the attempts at forcing someone to change are unsuccessful.

Always Being Right

People who tend to be perfectionists may experience this. This is the belief that we must be right or correct. Therefore, being wrong is unacceptable and we will do whatever we must to prove that we are right, even when we are wrong. Agreeing to disagree does not exist in those people's world and they may have destructive relationships, since they try to be right at all cost. Many times, they are also unable to admit mistakes, be fair, or be open to other views or beliefs.

Heaven's Reward Fallacy

This is the belief system that suffering and hard work is what will lead to a just reward. This may lead to some creating unnecessary suffering in their life. It can also lead to people getting frustrated when their hard work or suffering does not lead to the expected results. Sometimes no matter how hard you work on something or how much you suffer through a situation it will not lead to a reward or to achieve what you thought you would achieve. We can also think of it from the perspective of Karma and assume that if we do good that a reward or something good must occur. Good may occur, but if it does not meet our expectations or people do not react in ways that we expect, we may feel frustrated, angry and even depressed.

Mental Filter

Mental filters are very similar to overgeneralization. This is where a person may focus completely on one thing, such as the negative aspect of a situation, without being able to see the other sides, the positives. For example, a person may have a conversation and hear one negative thing that the other person said and then neglect to recognize or remember all the positive things that the person said. This tendency can lead us to only focus on the negative things around us. This can also happen if we have a bad thing happen to us in the morning and then expect that we are going to have a bad day because of it. We then filter out everything good in our day and only focus on negative things, which in the end proves our prediction correct and makes us feel like our bad morning ruined the whole day.

Disqualifying the Positive

On the other side we have disqualifying the positives, and this is when we DO recognize the positive but instead of accepting them we reject them. For example, if someone gives you a compliment, instead of accepting it we may feel that the person is just saying it to be nice to us and that they do not really mean it. This can lead us to develop a negative though habit in which we focus on the negatives even when positives are present or when we are presented with things that counter the negative.

4: R = RATIONAL: IRRATIONAL VS RATIONAL BELIEFS

The #1 goal of REBT is to change irrational beliefs into rational ones. Once the core limiting beliefs that are holding some back are disputed they can be replaced with new empowering ones. Other processes can be used to conquer irrational thoughts or emotional reactions at the surface, however dealing with the root of the problem—the underlying beliefs—is what makes lasting change possible. So, let's explore how to identify irrational beliefs and compare them to rational versions of the same beliefs.

Rational Belief	Irrational Belief
A rational belief is flexible For example: *"I want my co-worker to like me, but she does not have to"* This belief acknowledges what you want, which is for your co-worker to like you, but it is flexible because it also recognizes that you do not have to get what you want. It is not an absolute requirement or demand.	**An irrational belief is rigid** For example: *"My co-worker has to like me"* This belief doesn't just state what you want, it implies that it must be the case. You demand it. Because there is no flexibility, if she does not like you, you have no way of handling it.
A rational belief is non-extreme For example: *"It is bad if my co-worker doesn't like me, but it's not the end of the world"* This belief acknowledges that you find the situation negative, you think it's bad, but it also recognizes that it could be worse.	**An irrational belief is extreme** For example: *"It is the end of the world if my co-worker doesn't like me"* This belief is extreme because it expresses that you believe it could not be worse, when obviously it could be.
A rational belief is true Using the previous example: *"I want my co-worker to like me, but she does not have to like me."* Notice that this belief is made up of two parts: *"I want my co-worker to like me...."* *".... but she does not have to do so"* Part 1: Is it true? Can you prove it? Well, since it's your own desire, yes, you can confirm this. It's true. Part 2: Is it true? You can logically prove that the other person does not	**An irrational belief is false** Using the previous example: *"My co-worker has to like me."* Again, this belief is made up of two parts: *"I want my co-worker to like me...."* *".... and therefore she has to do so"* Part 1: Is it true? Can you prove it? Again, this is your own desire, so yes. Part 2: Is it true? You cannot prove in any way that your co-worker has

have to like you because otherwise you would be denying them free will. Both parts are true, therefore the belief is true.	to like you. She has freewill and therefore this cannot be true. It is false. Because both parts are not true, this belief is false.
A rational belief is sensible Does the belief "*I want my co-worker to like me, but she does not have to like me*" make sense? It does make sense because it's explicitly acknowledging that while you may want something that does not mean you have to get it.	**An irrational belief is not sensible** Does the belief "*My co-worker has to like me*" make sense? No, it does not make sense because it asserts that wanting something means you have to have it. The two are not connected.
A rational belief is largely constructive When beliefs are rational they are usually constructive, meaning they lead to beneficial consequences. For example, if you believe: "*I want my co-worker to like me, but she does not have to like me*" and then your co-worker snaps at you for no good reason, this belief will lead you to the following consequences: Emotional consequence: consequence: you'll be concerned about her response but not anxious about it. Behavioural consequence: If you address the situation with her, you will approach it in a reasonable way. Thinking consequence: While you may suspect that she may be upset with you, you will recognize it is likely she is upset with someone or something else and it has nothing to do with you.	**An irrational belief is largely unconstructive** When beliefs are irrational they are usually destructive, meaning they lead to negative consequences . For example, if you believe: "*My co-worker must like me*" and your co-worker snaps at you for no good reason, this belief will lead you to the following consequences: Emotional consequence: Her behaviour will make you anxious. Behavioural consequence: You are likely to either avoid her or try desperately to get her to like you. Thinking consequence: You will be certain that she is upset with you, rather than considering that there may be another reason for her behavior.

5: E = EMOTIVE: UNHEALTHY VS HEALTHY NEGATIVE EMOTIONS

It's common to hear people talk about negative and positive emotions. What most people are referring to is the fact that some emotions, such as happiness and excitement, are pleasant and others, like anger and sadness, are unpleasant. The problem arises when these different emotions are labelled good and bad. While happiness may feel good and sadness may feel bad, no emotions are entirely good or bad. If a psychopathic killer feels happy when they murder someone, would you say this is good? And if a person feels angry at themselves when they realize they did not take an opportunity they had been offered, and so they learn a lesson that will help them say yes to the next opportunity, is this bad?

Negative emotions may be unpleasant, but they are not bad, and labelling them that way will cause us to:

- Avoid situations that would elicit them
- Repress them when they do occur
- Judge ourselves or others for experiencing them

So, because emotions are not good or bad, it is more helpful to look at emotions as either healthy or unhealthy.

An **unhealthy negative emotion** is one that leads to unconstructive or harmful behavior or actions.

A **healthy negative emotion** is one that leads to constructive behavior or actions.

The truth about negative emotions is that each one of them has a healthy version and an unhealthy version. For example, anxiety is unhealthy but concern is healthy. Let's take a look at them now.

Anxiety vs Concern

Anxiety is a negative experience and it is unhealthy because it leads to unconstructive behaviors, such as:

- Withdrawing from the threat
- Avoiding the threat
- Seeking reassurance even though there is no way to get it
- Seeking safety from the threat

Of course, this may be justified if there is true danger, but what most people's brains label as a threat are minor life situations, such as someone saying something to us that makes us feel bad, having to experience uncertainty, or trying something new.

Concern, on the other hand, is a negative experience, yet it is healthy.

Concern leads to constructive behaviors, such as:
- Seeking to understand the threat
- Confronting the threat
- Seeking reassurance when it is possible

…which is usually reassuring themselves that the concern is only in their imagination and the likelihood of a truly negative outcome is very small.

Depression vs Sadness

Depression is a negative emotion that is unhealthy because it leads to prolonged withdrawal from enjoyable activities and it disrupts a person's ability to function in every-day-life.

Sadness, on the other hand, may feel negative but it is healthy because it leads a person to engage with enjoyable activities again after a brief period of mourning, loss, or unhappiness.

Guilt vs Remorse

Guilt is a negative emotion that is unhealthy because it leads to self-judgment, self-labelling as "bad", and often self-punishment. Due to feeling sorry for harm one inflicted, one may beg for forgiveness.

Remorse, on the other hand, may still feel negative, but it is healthy because it leads to acknowledgement of mistakes and taking responsibility for actions. Due to true empathy for the pain experienced by the other party, one may apologize and ask, but not beg for, forgiveness.

Shame vs Disappointment

Shame is a negative emotion that is unhealthy because it leads to withdrawal from others, avoiding eye contact, self-judgment, and self-punishment.

Disappointment, on the other hand, is a negative emotion that is healthy because it leads to keeping connection with others, maintaining eye contact, and acknowledging mistakes and taking responsibility for actions.

Hurt vs Sorrow

Hurt is a negative emotion that is unhealthy because it leads to sulking and withdrawal.

Sorrow is a negative emotion that is healthy because it leads to assertion and communicating with others.

Unhealthy Anger vs Healthy Anger

Unhealthy anger leads to aggression, both direct aggression and indirective or passive aggression.

Healthy anger leads to assertion and expression of concerns.

Unhealthy Jealousy vs Healthy Jealousy

Unhealthy jealousy leads to suspicion and prolonged questioning of the other party, checking in on them, and attempts at restricting them.

Healthy jealousy leads to reasonable, brief questioning of the other party and does not involve checking on or restricting the other them.

Unhealthy Envy vs Healthy Envy

Unhealthy envy leads to attempts to sabotage the other person's enjoyment of the desired possession or unhealthy feelings of anger or resentment toward the other party.

Healthy envy leads to striving to attain the desired possession for oneself, assuming it is truly desired, without any unhealthy feelings toward the other party.

6: B = BEHAVIOR: UNCONSTRUCTIVE VS CONSTRUCTIVE BEHAVIOR

In REBT behavior is defined as the actual action that is being taken by an individual, not just the thought. Irrational beliefs are what lead a person to irrational behaviors. When a behavior is irrational it is not constructive—it is harmful and leads to negative consequences. By developing rational beliefs, behaviors become constructive.

The reason this is so important is because there will always be situations in life that we could call adversity. The beliefs a person holds and the thoughts that they have about the situation will determine not only their emotional experience of it, but the behaviors they take and the resulting outcomes. Since adversity is inevitable, it is important to develop rational beliefs that help a person cope with adversity, choose constructive behaviors, and prevent unnecessary negative outcomes from situations that are already challenging.

So, put another way, when adversity happens and a person has irrational beliefs it leads to unconstructive behavior and when adversity happens and a person has rational beliefs it leads to constructive behavior.

If you want to change the behaviors, you need to change the belief.

Using the example we discussed in the Irrational vs Rational Beliefs chapter:

The adversity would be "My co-worker may not like me". The irrational belief would be "my co-worker must like me" and the unconstructive behavior would be avoiding of the co-worker or desperate attempts to get them to like me.

Looking at this same example but instead with a rational belief would look like this:

The adversity would be "my co-worker may not like me".

The rational belief would be "I want my co-worker like me, but she doesn't have to."

The constructive behavior would be directly asking the co-worker if there is anything wrong.

There are two great examples of ways irrational beliefs lead to unconstructive behaviors.

1. **Short-term Self-protective Behavior:** Using our example, imagine the belief was more general and applied to all co-workers. Now the person believes "everyone I work with must like me." Since their driving force is to be liked they may develop a self-protective behavior that seems to benefit them in the short term but that is unconstructive in the long term. Because of this deep need to be liked, the person will be hypersensitive to everyone they work with. They will try to prevent others from not liking them by going out of their way to try to be liked. While the effort may work to make the person feel liked in the short term, the long-

term unconstructive consequences would be preventing themselves from learning how the other people would treat them without being manipulated into appearing to like the person, as well as inauthentic relationships. Another possible long-term outcome would be causing the exact situation they fear by because even while smothering co-workers with kindness in attempt at being liked, the anxiety about being accepted would show through with behavior such as being guarded, defensive, or even avoiding social contact.

2. **Over-compensatory Behavior:** Another common unconstructive behavior that is triggered by irrational beliefs is the tendency to over-compensate for what the person fears. This means that the person is trying to prove themselves wrong about what they think is the truth about them, other people, or themselves. For example, if a person believes "I will not be able to deal with this obstacle", they will take on a greater obstacle in order to prove to themselves that they can, in fact, handle the original challenge or obstacle.

Another common example is workaholism. If a person believes "if I am not a high achiever I am defective, inferior, and will be rejected" they will work excessively in attempt at proving their status, success and self-worth. Unfortunately, because the underlying belief and fear is always there, no matter how much they achieve, they continue to feel the same way, which is shameful and unworthy.

Now, this doesn't mean that all workaholism is due to a need at proving a person's worth. Other times, overworking can be a coping strategy to avoid failure in another area. For example, a person who is struggling in their marriage may work excessively to avoid dealing with the failure of the marriage. They may hold an underlying irrational belief, such as "I cannot get divorced and if I do I am a failure and a bad person." This belief leads to the unconstructive behavior of over-working.

Another example is a person who is over-controlling of loved ones. The irrational belief they hold is that "people cannot be trusted" because they have experienced abuse, neglect, or extreme let down in their past. This belief leads to the behavior of being highly suspicious of others and actively manipulating or controlling them in attempt at preventing the possibility of being hurt.

The final example is a person who is rebellious. The irrational belief they hold is that "authority figures will dominate, bully, or control me." This belief leads to the behavior of rebelling against the desires and directives of authority figures in attempt at proving that they are autonomous and will not be controlled. They do this to avoid feeling hopeless or trapped.

7: INTELLECTUAL VS. EMOTIVE UNDERSTANDING

Even once you can identify that a belief is irrational, that the emotion is unhealthy, and that the resulting behavior is unconstructive, this doesn't necessarily mean you'll have the ability to change the emotion or the behavior to be constructive.

You see, there is a difference between understanding something at an intellectual level versus understanding it at an emotional level.

When a person is trying to transform an irrational belief into a rational one, it is important to recognize that simply understanding that the belief is rational is not enough to change it. For example, you may have a belief that your co-worker must like you. You may be able to rationalize with yourself and acknowledge that the belief is not rational. However, when your co-worker snaps at you, you still react emotionally by feeling anxious and you still behave based on the irrational belief by avoiding this co-worker.

We've all had experiences when we've known that our beliefs—such as our fears—make no sense logically, but we still feel afraid and act accordingly.

The only way to actually adopt the rational belief that your co-workers do not have to like you is to understand it at an emotional level. When you understand things at an emotive level you are also able to feel and behave differently. When you get to this point, thinking the new, rational, belief makes you feel better. It eases your anxiety. You may still feel negative emotions, such as concern, but you won't feel anxious or have a need to avoid your co-worker. You'll also easily transition at that point to other rational beliefs, such as "my co-worker may not be upset at me and may have other things bothering them."

Getting to the point of emotive understanding, when a new rational belief causes an emotional shift and changes behavior, can take time, repetition, and different processes. All of the REBT tools and strategies in the rest of this book are used to help develop this shift from intellectually understanding that our thinking is irrational to actually believing it and feeling the shift.

8: THE THREE LEVELS OF THINKING

REBT looks at three levels of thinking and they are:
- Inferences
- Evaluations
- Core Beliefs

Inferences

This level of thinking identifies "what is happening". Your mind processes what is happening around you and makes an assumption based on what you know, which may be limited, and whether it meets your expectations and demands. You then take your conclusion as a fact. This interpretation and perspective about reality all happens automatically and in a split second.

Evaluations

This level of thinking identifies "what does it mean?" Based on what your mind concludes about what is happening, it then evaluates the situation to determine what it means. It goes beyond simply the fact of reality, it assigns meaning to it. your needs and rules are met, it labels it good. If they're unmet, it labels it bad. And, depending on this final judgment, we will feel good or bad.

Core Beliefs

This level of thinking identifies "how life should be" and it exists at the unconscious level. In fact, all 3 levels of thinking are usually unconscious, however the beliefs or rules are the deepest level, meaning we're totally unaware we hold these beliefs. In REBT we look at the interference and evaluations, which are easier to identify, in order to figure out the core beliefs that drive the assumptions and judgments. The beliefs we hold about how life should be can be thought of as musts or demands. They are the rules we've developed for ourselves that tell us how we

NEED things to be in life. One example could be that we believe we need to be approved of by others in order to be worthy.

The evaluation level of thinking is where our power lies to create change. Normally, this assigning of meaning and the resulting emotional response, again, happens automatically and unconsciously. However, by becoming aware of our emotional reactions or disturbances, as well as knowing the faulty way our minds tend to evaluate life situations so you can avoid them, we can choose constructive, rational ways of assigning meaning to events.

In the next section, we will dive deeper into understanding our human needs and beliefs, what types of beliefs lead to emotional disturbances, the dysfunctional ways we tend to assign meaning to situations, and the 3 core rules or musts that are the core of most of our irrational thinking and emotional pain.

And then in the rest of the book we'll dive into processes that will help make this entire process of thinking and interpreting our world CONSCIOUS, so we have more control over what we think and the emotions we experience because of it. We will learn how to develop awareness of emotional disturbances and questioning the meaning we assign them. We'll learn how to question our perception and assumptions and rewire the underlying beliefs that are the core of the problem.

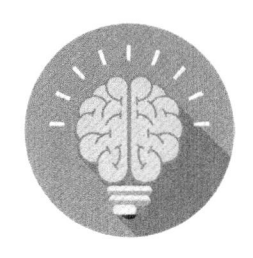

SECTION 4: DEVELOPING AWARENESS OF THOUGHTS, EMOTIONS, AND BEHAVIORS

1: CULTIVATING MINDFULNESS AND SELF-AWARENESS

"The outer situation of your life and whatever happens there is the surface of the lake. Sometimes calm, sometimes windy and rough, according to the cycles and seasons. Deep down, however, the lake is always undisturbed. You are the whole lake, not just the surface." – Eckhart Tolle

For most people, the chaos and noise happening around them and within their own minds feels like all there is. They live in a constant state of reactivity, being pushed and pulled by the thoughts and emotions they experience. They're controlled by a voice in their head that worries about everything that can go wrong, criticizes them for everything they do wrong, and feels guilty or angry about everything that went wrong. This voice interprets every situation instantaneously and we don't question it, just like we don't question our breathing. It all happens unconsciously, meaning we are unaware of it. And then we feel and act based on the voice's interpretation.

The truth is that everyone has a voice in their head, including you.

Some people's voices are nicer than others, but everyone's voice tends to have the same disfunctions. But the good news—perhaps the best news anyone can ever hear is that this voice is not who you are.

For some of the people reading this book, you already know this well. For others, it may be the first time you have heard it, or the first time you truly understand it. If you've ever argued with yourself over something or you've ever noticed yourself thinking about something ridiculous or you've ever talked to yourself in your own mind, then you've experienced that there are two of you. There is the one that does the thinking, feeling, and reacting and there is the one that is aware of the thoughts, emotions, and reactions. You are that awareness. You are the presence that witnesses the voice, but you are not the voice.

Knowing this allows you to observe what your inner voice is doing and thinking. This is called self-observation or self-awareness. As you become more and more aware of what has always been going on unconsciously, beneath the surface of your awareness, you become conscious. You wake up from the dream. And the process for developing this awareness is called mindfulness.

Until you develop self-awareness and mindfulness, you will likely live much of your life on auto pilot, feeling like you have little control over your thoughts, emotions, or life. The truth is that unless you know what you're thinking, feeling, or doing, you have no way of changing it.

Simply developing this awareness is the key that unlocks all of your power. Power to direct your own inner voice, choose better-feeling emotions, and making better decisions.

Start by listening to the voice in your head as often as you can. Pay particular attention to any thoughts that repeat. Be the observer of what is happening inside of you—both the surface of the lake and the depths. See if you can find and feel the deep calm at the bottom of the lake even when the surface is rough.

As you practice mindfulness and observing your thoughts and reactions, you'll be able to recognize even more clearly that the presence doing the observing is the true you. When you notice yourself feeling angry, you'll observe that the angry part and the part observing it are not the same thing. This is important to know because your true self never becomes disrupted and entangled in these surface level dramas. There is a part of you that is at peace, content, safe, and joyful no matter what is going on around you and in your mind. Your higher self is untouchable, un-disruptable. Knowing it is always there means you can seek to find it in any moment.

And, just like when the sun dips below the horizon you know that it still exists, even though you cannot see it, this calm, peaceful presence that is you is always there, even if you cannot see it.

As you begin to pay attention with a sense of curiosity to discover what your inner voice is up to, you'll begin to notice interesting things it does. You'll notice when you are behaving in a way that is in alignment with our goals and our values, and when you are not. You'll notice when you are smiling even though you are actually sad, or when you say you are fine even though you are not. You may notice you are pretending to be mad when you really aren't, just to manipulate someone else's behavior. Or, you may notice that you are thinking negative thoughts about yourself, making you feel insecure. You may even notice when we are soothing yourself or feeling relaxed or happy.

The last thing you need to know about cultivating mindfulness before we move on is that the doorway to all awareness is the present moment. Most people's minds have a strong habit of spending a lot of time thinking about the past or imagining, and usually worrying about, the future. But, the power to observe and redirect your thoughts, emotions, and behaviors is only accessible when you are focused on the present moment. When you're paying attention to what is going on in this moment, you can notice the mind remembering an experience from the past or worrying about the future. But, if yourself to go with your mind TO these past or future places, you lose your sense of awareness. For this reason, one excellent way to develop mindfulness and self-awareness is to pay attention as often as you can to what is happening RIGHT NOW. Pay attention to each step you take, to the noises going on around you, to your breathing. Once you pull your awareness back into the present moment, it gives you an opportunity to notice what you're thinking.

It is also important for you to know that the next time you notice yourself experiencing a negative thought or emotion, it doesn't mean you've failed—it means you've succeeded! Until you are able to become aware of these negative experiences you have little power over them. So, every time you notice a negative thought, celebrate! Give yourself a high five! Because now you know that this negative thought is NOT who you are. You are the one in charge and you will be spending the rest of this book learning how to develop this awareness and use proven tools to change the content of your inner world.

2: DEVELOPING AWARENESS OF YOUR THOUGHTS AND SELF-TALK

There are two layers of thoughts—the ones we can hear or experience as the voice in our head, that makes commentary about ourselves and everything around us, and the deeper level beliefs that determine our opinions, perspectives, and judgments.

CBT primarily focuses on the first category, and specifically on self-talk, which is the part of your inner voice's chatter directed at ourselves. Our self-talk can be an inner cheerleader that motivates and sooths, or it can be an inner critic that is harsh and self-defeating. Our self-talk impacts how we feel about ourselves as well as how we behave and is ultimately responsible for our experience of life and the outcomes that occur because of our actions.

For instance, you may have heard of the concept of a self-fulfilling prophecy, which is a psychological concept that basically means that we will live up to our own expectations or create the situations we expect. For instance, if you are constantly telling yourself you're a failure, it impacts the way you feel—discouraged, self-doubt, anxiety—which impacts how you act and the choices you make. Either you'll make poor choices, like deciding not to try, or when you do take actions, you'll give half-hearted effort. Why bother? You're going to fail anyway, right? In the end, you fail. But it's not because you're a failure, it's because of your thinking.

The deeper level beliefs you hold about yourself, others, the world are what causes your inner voice to talk to you, about you, the way it does. One important thing to know is that you were not born with either a cheerleader voice or a critic voice—you learned how to think this way. How? By observing the way your caretakers and others talked about themselves, about others, and about you. You weren't born fearing failure. When you were a toddler you made a mistake and just kept right on going, that is, until an adult acted like falling down was the end of the world or shamed you for doing something "wrong". Over time, that external voice becomes your internal voice. If you're a parent, think honestly for a second about what you have programmed your child's inner voice to say to them. Ouch, I know.

So, if you just realized that you have programmed some limiting and harsh self-talk into your children, and you're realizing that you've probably been programmed this way too, there is good news: WE CAN ALL BE REPROGRAMMED.

By becoming aware of your self-talk, the positive and the negative, you can CHANGE IT. Self-talk is simply a habit of thinking. So, start out by considering the general predisposition of your inner voice. What percentage of the time do you think your inner voice falls into these 3 categories:

1. Criticize yourself, put yourself down, talk negatively to yourself
2. Make excuses, blame others, tell yourself it's not your fault
3. Tell yourself it will be okay, encourage yourself to learn from the situation

There is nothing right or wrong about your answer to this. Everyone has an inner cheerleader and an inner critic, however the vast majority of people have a very dominant inner critic. This negative side of your thinking can present itself in a variety of ways, which we'll get into in a moment. This is like the fixed mindset persona, but in its full form.

Before we move on, I want to make sure that you always remember that your inner critic is NOT you. So, take a moment and give it a name (you can use the same name you created for your fixed mindset persona).

Inner critic name: _____

We like to call ours "Bob"!

Negative Self-Talk Triggers

In the last chapter you named your inner critic. (Like we mentioned, we like to call ours Bob.) There are 4 common and easy-to-spot ways that your inner critic shines it's light of negativity on your world. Try to catch it in the act. When you notice it thinking one of these types of negative thoughts, simply observe it. Don't judge it or criticize it because if you do, it's just the same inner critic voice coming in the back door again. Think about that one—now you have 2 Bobs! Yikes!

1. **Self-Limiting.** When my Bob is trying to limit me, he says things like "it's too hard, I can't do this" or "it's too risky" or "I don't have time". Ultimately, Bob likes making excuses. This is even more common if you lean toward having a fixed mindset, like we discussed already. When you believe your abilities are fixed and you believe failing means you are a failure, the best way to avoid humiliation is to not try at all—which is what excuses are for, aren't they? Your Bob tries to shut down possibilities and solutions before you even get started.

2. **Assumptions.** Bob's believe they're always right and that they're psychic. They like to think they can read other people's minds and assume what they're thinking and feeling. They like to jump to conclusions and make snap judgments. The Fact or Opinion activity is great if your Bob likes to assume things. Look out for your Bob saying things like "everyone will talk about me", I made a fool out of myself", "she doesn't like me". Your inner critic is making up stories that aren't even true. Once you know this, you won't fall for it so easily.

3. **Re-runs.** Most of our self-talk happens on autopilot. Our repetitive, automatic thoughts have been going on for so long we don't even notice them. Chances are your Bob says things all the time that you don't even actually believe, but you let him get away with it because you're so used it. Often these habits of thought become habits of speech, so you may even catch yourself saying these things to others, out loud. So, be on the lookout for 2 things:
   1. **Thoughts**, especially memories or anticipated events, that tend to replay a scene in your mind over and over again, like a mini-movie on re-run.
   2. **Phrases you say to yourself or others repeatedly,** especially if they are making a judgement about yourself.

   For example: "I'm always late" or "I'm an idiot" or "here we go again" or "this always happens to me".

4. **Others' Thoughts.** Sometimes your Bob is simply parroting someone else. You will be shocked when you realize how many of the thoughts that go through your mind are NOT your own. It is time to GET OTHER PEOPLE OUT OF YOUR HEAD. Like we already mentioned, your inner dialog has been programmed throughout your life. Your nagging mom now takes up residence in your mind. The good news, is you can kick her out! The key for this one is to look question the thoughts you have about what you "should" or "shouldn't" do. These words are a sign that the belief behind them was planted by someone else. If YOU actually believed it, in most cases you wouldn't be telling yourself you SHOULD do it, you'd just simply do it.

- Ask yourself, "Who's voice am I hearing?"
- Do I really believe that I "should" do this? (Hint, if you're feeling a sense of guilt, it's probably not your own, original, belief.)
- If yes, make it a MUST and do it.
- If not—if this is someone else hijacking your mind, tell them to GET OUT and then ask yourself, what do I really believe?

What's Your Inner Critic's Personality

So, you've named your inner critic so you don't take it so personally and you've learned what to look out for in order to get good at noticing your negative thinking. Now, let's look at 4 common personality types that your inner critic may have. Understanding the way your inner critic tends to think will help you identify what you can do to tame it.

The worrier: Points out everything that can go wrong. Stirs up emotions of anxiety and fear by imagining disasters, expecting the worst, and overestimating the odds of something bad happening. It tends to say "what if"? If your Bob is a Worrier, you can tame it by focusing on the activities in this program that will help ease stress and re-assure your Bob, such as meditation, breathing, visualization, and exposure techniques.

The critic: Constantly judges and evaluates your behavior and points out your flaws. Jumps on any mistake you make and reminds you of past failures. Compares you to others and assumes they will judge you. It even minimizes your accomplishments! It tends to say "you're an idiot". If your Bob is a Critic, you can tame it by focusing on the activities in this program that will help you retrain your thought patterns, such as cognitive distortions, Socratic questioning, and the growth mindset.

The victim: It tells you that you're hopeless, not making progress, or that it's too hard. It tells you there is something wrong with you, your incapable, unworthy. You're not smart enough. There are too many obstacles in your way. It's not your fault. It tends to say "I can't". If your Bob is a Victim, you can tame it by focusing on the activities in this program that will help you take your power back, such as the growth mindset section.

The perfectionist: It pushes you to do better but even when you do better you still feel like you're not good enough. There is always more you should be doing. Mistakes and setbacks must be avoided or quickly moved past. It pushes you to seek external validation, achievement, status. Acceptance by others is of the utmost importance. It probably even stops you from taking action because you're afraid to fail. Tends to say "I need to do better" or "I'm not good enough". If your Bob is a Perfectionist, you can tame it by focusing on the activities in this program that will help you judge yourself less, such as the growth mindset section, overcoming indecision, and overcoming inaction.

Take Your Power Back from Bob

Now that you know what to look out for so you can notice your inner critic in action, go out into the world and practice observing it. When you catch your Bob in the act, use the following 3 strategies to take your power back from these negative thoughts.

- **Ignore Bob:** Don't take Bob seriously. When Bob starts rambling on incessantly or hops on a negative train, imagine Bob has a funny voice or is wearing a clown suit. Bob is not you, and it doesn't know what it's talking about.

- **Protect Bob:** Bob's easily influenced, so always ask yourself if YOU really believe what it's saying. We already talked about getting people out of your head. One way to do this is pay special attention for any thoughts coming from Bob that sound eerily similar to things other people say (such as your parents, the media, authority figures). Choose what you expose Bob to wisely, because he's apt to believe it and repeat it.

- **Observe Bob:** As often as you can, remind yourself to watch your Bob. Notice what it's thinking about. If you don't like what it's thinking about, CHOOSE A NEW THOUGHT. You're in charge. Many of the activities discussed throughout this book are designed to help you observe, record, and re-direct your Bob.

Remember that it takes time to get good at keeping your Bob in check. You'll notice times when Bob runs off on a tangent of terrible thoughts without you noticing—sneaky Bob! But no worries because when you eventually notice what Bob is doing you can WHACK Bob on the head—it's like playing Whack-a-Mole. Whack him and say "bad Bob!" and laugh. This stops the negative thought, giving you a moment to remember that you have a choice. You can then implement one of the thought-changing strategies you learn in the book and pick a better thought. The more you observe your Bob the better you'll get at catching it in the act—and as you practice, the voice will get quieter and your inner cheerleader will take the lead.

3: DEVELOPING AWARENESS OF YOUR EMOTIONS

Sometimes people have a difficult time identifying their emotions and it's usually because of one of the following reasons:
- We were made to think our feelings don't matter
- We were made to fear expressing our emotions
- We were made to feel guilty if our emotions (or desires) were an inconvenience on others
- We were discouraged from feeling or expressing specific emotions

Because of our conditioning, some people stop expressing their emotions and often repress them (hold them in). Other people go a step further and stop allowing themselves to have them. In either case, this can lead to a lessened ability to recognize how they feel.

Even people who did not learn to repress or turn off certain emotions—even if they feel things deeply—they can simply not have ever been taught about their emotions and so they cannot clearly identify them. Their emotions feel overwhelming and out-of-control.

If you want to re-gain your power to direct your own emotional state, you need to be able to:
- Notice you're experiencing an emotional state

- Identify what it is
- Know what to expect
- Know how to influence a new emotional state

Emotional States

Emotional States are actually 2 different things:
- The STATE is the physiological "feelings" that you experience
- The EMOTION is the psychological interpretation or "label" you put on the state

We experience complex states made up of chemical and hormone interactions that cause a variety of reactions in the body. Our emotions are the interpretations we make of these experiences—or the labels we give them.

So, based on what we talked about in Thoughts Create Emotions, we need to add a couple steps to the process.

Situation → Interpretation (thought) → State → Interpretation (label) → Emotion

What this means is the body responds to the thought first, then our minds interpret the reaction, label it, and an emotion is born.

We can have physiological feelings that aren't emotions. We can feel hot, cold, nauseous, or energetic. But, when we interpret them to have meaning, we turn them into emotions.

Emotions literally mean action: e-MOTION. Each emotional state is designed to get us to do something, and often we do. Our emotional state affects our behavior, but it does not cause it. When we're angry we're more likely to be aggressive, but our cognitive (thought) processes allow us to make those decisions.

The Map is Not the Territory

The labels we give emotions are like a box or a map. What's printed on the box may signal what's inside, but it is NOT what is inside. Just like a map may describe a territory, however it is NOT the territory. Maps are simplified, inadequate and ultimately flawed. It would be like eating a menu. In the same way, what we call "anger", the word, is not the experience. Saying you "love" someone hardly does the experience any justice. In fact, all words are simply signposts pointing toward meaning. The word "tree" is not a tree.

So, what IS an emotion if it's not a map? Well, it's not a "thing" either. You see, labeling an experience as an emotion makes it seem like a NOUN. This is why many people believe emotions are things they HAVE or that happen TO them. The truth is that emotions are verbs (emoting is the verb)—they are a PROCESS. Fear is the process of fearing, which is a string of sensations that occur in a pattern. Fear takes many steps from observation or contemplation to processing and interpreting; then to physiological reaction and FEELING, and finally labeling it as fear.

If you obscure the process underneath a word label, you end up believing that emotions aren't under your conscious control. Once we recognize anger is a process, we recognize we have power over it.

Emotion Identification Chart:

Below are 6 common emotions and descriptions of the emotion, physiological state, and common resulting behaviors. This chart will help you get a general idea of the signs and symptoms of each emotion to make them easier to identify; specifically, easier to identify early. Everyone experiences each emotion somewhat differently and you may not experience all of the characteristics.

LABEL	EMOTION	STATE	BEHAVIOR
Happiness	Intense, positive feelings of well-being, pleasure, contentment, delight, joy, optimism, and gratitude. Affirmative, positive thoughts and mental clarity.	Head held high (posture), wide-eyed, smiling, laughing, relaxation of muscles, open body language.	Pleasant voice, friendly, swinging arms, dancing.
Boredom	Low-intensity, unpleasant feelings of apathy, restlessness, indifference, empty-ness, and frustration. Defeatist thinking or wishing things were different.	Low energy, slumped posture, smirk or frown, low eyes, shallow breathing.	Resting head, fidgeting, staring.
Anxiety	Vague, unpleasant feelings of distress, uneasiness, stress, apprehension, and nervousness. Thoughts of uncertainty and worry, racing thoughts, difficulty concentrating and remembering.	Restlessness, sweating, clammy hands, hunched shoulders, swallowing, quickened breath, darting eyes, butterflies in the stomach, nausea.	Pacing, biting lip, fidgeting. Irritability, hypervigilance.
Anger	Intense, uncomfortable feelings of hostility and hurt. Feeling out of control. Thoughts of blame and resentment. Difficulty thinking clearly or rationally.	Muscle tension, headache, tight chest, increased heart rate, increased blood pressure, heavy breathing, clenched fist, furrowed brow, showing teeth, clenched jaw, sweating, trembling, flushed cheeks, large posture.	Loud voice, yelling, cursing, sarcasm, pacing. Sometimes leads to aggression, including hitting a wall, throwing an object, or lashing out at a person.
Sadness/ Depression	Feelings of intense pain and sorrow, guilt, un-worthiness, disappoint-ment, helplessness, gloominess, loss, grief, numbness, meaninglessness, loss of interest. Defeated thinking and difficulty concentrating and remembering.*	Slumped posture and hunched shoulders, long face, slow movements, pouting, body aches, crying, shaking, crossed arms, fatigue, upset stomach, monotone voice.	Curling up into a ball, laying around, withdrawing, irritability.
Fear	Intense feeling of dread, impending doom, or panic due to a perceived danger or threat. Paranoid or worst-case thinking and hyper focused on the object of the fear.	Increased heart rate, increased blood pressure, alert eyes, high eyebrows, corners of cheeks pulled toward ears, clammy, sweating, quickened breath, goose bumps, butterflies in the stomach, shaky voice.	Freezing, fleeing, hiding.

*Depression is a long-term period of sadness that is caused by more than a psychological reaction to circumstances. Depression is a real and serious condition and needs to be treated by a medical professional.

Practicing Emotional Awareness and Identification

Next time you catch yourself experiencing an emotion that is distinct, ask yourself the following questions. Practice this line of questioning often, especially when experiencing unpleasant emotions.

- How do I feel?
- How do I know?
- What do I feel? Sensations?
- Where do I feel it? Locations?
- Where in my body did it begin? Move to?
- How do I recognize when OTHERS experience this emotion?
- Do I notice any of these signs in myself?
- What do I observe in my body language, vocal tone, thoughts, behaviors?

4: SITUATIONAL VS. PSYCHOLOGICAL FEAR

Situational Fear

If our bodies didn't have a natural stress response we would be dead. Actually, our ancestors would have died and we never would have been born at all. Our fight-or-flight response was designed to save our cave-dwelling ancestors from an untimely death in the jaws of a saber-toothed predator or other danger. Our bodies increase our heart rate and send a flood of adrenaline and cortisol throughout our bodies, getting oxygen to the brain and energy to the muscles. This "fear response" provides us an instinctive form of self-protection, allowing us to flee dangerous situations or muster the strength to defend ourselves. *This is situational fear—fear that is triggered by an immediate threat in our current situation.*

It's true that instinctual fear is healthy. It keeps us safe. But many people give fear too much merit—they believe that by living in a state of fear they're somehow protecting themselves and their loved ones. But unless you're under immediate threat, fear is completely unnecessary. You don't need fear to avoid danger – just a minimum of intelligence and common sense. For example, the reason you don't put your hand in the fire is not because of fear. It's because you know that you'll get burned. When a child touches a hot stove and gets burned, they learn that fire equals pain.

They learn to avoid touching fire. There is no fear involved.

Now, as an adult this person may be in a home that catches fire—and it would be natural for them to become fearful. The resulting fight or flight response would help them quickly and safely exit the burning building. However, if this person, as a child or an adult, develops a "fear of fire"—meaning when they think about fire they become frightened—they are experiencing psychological fear, not real fear.

Psychological fear

Psychological fear is divorced from any concrete and true immediate danger. It is always fear of something that might happen.

The problem is that while you can always cope with the present moment, you cannot cope with something that is only in your imagination. This is the reason many people report that the thing they were afraid of, when they finally actually experienced it, wasn't "as bad as they expected".

Here is an example of how real fear is different than psychological fear and why the latter is harder to deal with. If you were driving and notice out of the corner of your eye that a car is about to hit you, your body responds, and you enter the fear response. The car swerves and danger is diverted. If this has ever happened to you, immediately after the situation you likely noticed your heart was beating in your chest and your breathing was heavy. You may have noticed your palms were clammy or that you felt shaky. But, since it's over, your mind says, "it's okay now" and your body begins to calm down. Within a couple minutes you're back to normal.

This is because the chemicals and hormones and heart rate we experience in order to save our lives are supposed to return to normal after our Neanderthal is sitting around the cave fire telling his buddies about his narrow miss. But in the modern world our bodies don't normalize because our stress isn't caused by threat of death. For us, everything looks like a toothed predator! Our stress is constant! Overbearing bosses, tight schedules, nagging children, distant spouses, and empty hearts put many of us in a state of chronic worry, anxiety and stress.

Our habit of worrying puts us on edge. Then, a stressful situation can agitate us further, adding to the tension we already had and causing physiological reactions, such as increased heart rate, high blood pressure. If we continue to focus on the "problem" causing our state of anxiety, it gets worse. We feel out of control. Our body fully enters the state of fight or flight. And, here's the key... because there is no REAL THREAT happening our mind cannot say "here is the danger and this is what you can do to protect yourself." And because it's not real, your mind cannot stop it and then say "it's over, I'm okay now." The mind, who is trying to protect you, then looks at this fear response and thinks "there must be something wrong." It escalates the situation and you begin to panic. You think there's something wrong with you. You may even think you're dying. You're under attack, but the assailant is YOU.

This is psychological fear, and although the experience is very real, what you are afraid of is imaginary.

You are fighting a battle with a phantom shadow.

The best way to win this battle with psychological fear is to stop it before it starts. Remind yourself that it's not real and that you have the power to stop yourself from spiraling into a state of fear. Catch yourself when you're feeling stressed, uncertain or anxious and take action to change your situation, environment or mental focus to help you de-escalate your emotional state.

5: IDENTIFYING TRIGGERS

We all have triggers, both positive and negative. They can be conscious or unconscious. When they are conscious they can be easily identified. More obvious or conscious triggers include: a specific conversation topic, a person, a song, a smell or anything else that we *know* makes us emotional or react a certain way. The biggest challenge we have when addressing our triggers is the fact that most of them are unconscious—meaning we are not aware they are happening.

For example, you may be having a conversation or doing something and you get mad, defensive, or anxious for no apparent reason. You aren't aware of what made you feel that way and so often you blame the person you're talking to or the situation you're in, when the real reason for your reaction is that the situation triggered a learned reaction in your brain. It can be frustrating, however it's important to keep in mind that these triggers were originally created by our brain as a way to help us be efficient with our responses to the world around us and, ultimately, to keep us safe.

Like we talked about in the "You Can Change Your Brain" chapter, our brain becomes wired when we're exposed to something repeatedly. But, another way something becomes strongly wired is when we have an experience that is highly emotional. When we're emotional, our brains assume 2 things:

1. Whatever going on at the time is the cause of the emotion
2. Remembering that this thing is associated with this emotion is important

Once the situation—the place, person, or thing—is programmed into the brain with a certain emotion attached to it, this same thing becomes a trigger, meaning the next time you find yourself with that place, person, or thing, it automatically triggers that same emotion.

The best example is music. If you've ever listened to a song while experiencing emotional situations in your life, that song will forever trigger the emotion to come back when you listen to it in the future. This is why that song you listened and cried when your girl or boyfriend broke up with you still makes your heart ache or why your favorite high school anthem still pumps you up.

Unfortunately, sometimes our brain creates an association between the emotion and a person, place or thing that is NOT truly the cause. When this mis-association happens, the faulty wiring can do more harm than good. For example, if your parents told you "we need to talk" every time just before you got in trouble, then in the future if a friend or spouse says "we need to talk" you'll immediately become defensive. You aren't aware of the real reason you feel that way, and so you blame your friend.

The key to recognizing your negative triggers is to become a student of your own emotions—especially when the emotion does not seem to fit the situation. By becoming aware of triggers, you start to take their power away because you can choose to react differently, instead of reacting automatically.

Ask yourself, what tends to trigger me emotionally Then, for each one, consider in what way you react to those triggers and whether the reaction is appropriate or reasonable. Lastly, for each trigger, ask yourself: How could I react differently? How could I think differently? Feel differently? Act differently?

Developing Awareness of Thoughts, Emotions, and Behaviors

Emotional Trigger	My Reaction	Reasonable? Yes or No	How Could I React Differently?

Other questions to help you identify triggers:
- What people trigger me? What do they do or say? What do I think as a response? How do I feel or act? Is it reasonable? What could be different?
- What topics of conversation trigger me? Why? How do I feel or act? What could be different?
- What places do I go that tend to trigger me? What do I think, feel or act? What could be different?

Below are additional common triggers to give you ideas for what to look for:
- Having to make a change
- Challenging yourself or learning something new
- Being criticized
- Failing at something
- When something goes wrong
- When you make a mistake
- When you make a mistake in front of others
- Being put on the spot
- When you procrastinate
- When you're on a deadline, pressured, or rushed
- When your reputation is at risk
- What other triggers can you think of?

6: IDENTIFYING UNDERLYING BELIEFS

Beneath all of your thoughts and behaviors are beliefs that influence you. A belief is just a thought you've thought enough times that you believe it or that was taught to you forcefully enough or that was developed because of an experience you had. Once you believe something to be true, you make assumptions. You make decisions based on what you believe. Your thoughts are directed in the direction of what you believe. But, a belief is just a well-habituated thought. The truth is that a very large percentage of what you believe to be true is, in fact, false. But, you live out your entire life based on these beliefs. We could do a whole book just on evaluating and changing your beliefs, but learning how to direct your thoughts is the best place to start.

You probably believe that no two finger prints are alike, lightning won't strike the same place twice, dropping a penny from a tall building and hitting someone below will kill someone, cracking your knuckles gives you arthritis and it takes 7 years to digest swallowed chewing gum. But none of these are true. The reason you believe them is you were taught it by people who you thought knew more than you and you just continued to think it. Well, now you know it's all wrong. You're welcome!

But, these are just silly, unimportant things you assumed were true… now imagine how many other false beliefs you are carrying around with you! The problem with false beliefs is that they limit you. You make all of your decisions based on what you know, or what you think you know. So if you're wrong, you are potentially missing out on options you didn't know you had. You might be making judgments based on inaccurate information. And these faulty beliefs have real consequences.

Where many coaches, therapists, or people using CBT on themselves make a mistake is they use the techniques to change thinking patterns and redirect emotions in the moment, but they never dig deep enough to uncover the underlying belief that is causing it in the first place.

You might be thinking about how rude and ungrateful your sister is for asking you to babysit AGAIN when you just did two days ago. You're thinking "doesn't she know I have a life? I have things I need to do." You're feeling angry and you're directing it at her. You may be able to change your thinking and focus on the fact that she doesn't normally ask for so much help. This is an exception because everyone in her family has been sick with the flu over the last week and she has things she hasn't been able to take care of. Changing your thinking helps you change your perspective, develop compassion and release your anger. But, it doesn't address the underlying belief that was causing you to react that way in the first place.

The underlying belief was probably the belief that if someone asks for your help you are obligated to say yes. The true source of the anger was not at your sister for asking, it was because of your dislike of the feeling of obligation. You were mad at yourself for not knowing how to honor yourself and say no. By identifying and addressing the underlying belief, you can make permanent changes, rather than simply changing the thought and emotion in the moment. You can really look at the belief that you are obligated to help when asked and create a healthier definition for yourself about what it means to be supportive to others, while at the same time honoring yourself. You can develop strategies for setting boundaries, making it easier to say no when you need to AND develop better patterns of thinking about it so that in the future when you agree to help someone, you recognize that it was truly your choice and you do not feel obligated or bitter about it.

To get to the root belief that's beneath your thinking, go through the following questions. You can also combine this activity with other CBT activities to make sure you root out the core of the problem rather than continuing to have to face the same negative beliefs over and over again.

When you identify a negative thought, especially if it is one that you've had over and over again, ask yourself:

- What is the thought I am thinking?

- Who or what is it directed at?

- How do I feel about it?

- Why do I feel that way?

- What do I believe should be different? What rule is it breaking?

- What is the belief?

- What would you have to assume or believe in order to believe this?

- Is there a deeper belief or fear beneath this?

- When is the first time I remember having this thought and feeling this way?

- What experience did I have that caused me to believe this?

- Could you have misinterpreted it? Was there another perspective or other information you may have missed?

- Who do I know that thinks this way or expressed this belief to me?

- What benefits did they receive from believing it or telling you to believe it?

- Are they right? How do you know?

- Keep probing and asking yourself until you get to the core of the belief, then summarize the core, underlying belief.

- On a scale of 1 to 10, 10 being true with 100% certainty, how certain are you that this belief is true?

- How do you know?

- What other possibilities can you think of that might be true instead?

- What would you like to believe instead?

- How does thinking this new belief make you feel?

Thinking back to the original negative thought and the reason behind it, how has how you feel about it changed?

You can dig even further into a process for changing a limiting or false belief and building up a strong new empowering belief to replace it with the Changing Beliefs activity.

7: A NOTE ABOUT ACCEPTANCE

We have mentioned this throughout the book, but it is worth repeating how important it is to accept your thoughts and emotions as they are.

It is 100% normal to have negative, self-deprecating, limited, or even scary thoughts. Once a thought is focused on long enough, it starts to pull additional, similar thoughts from your memory, as well as see more and more of what you're thinking about around you. This momentum can get you stuck on a train of thinking that can feel like it's going out of control.

At the same time, it is 100% normal to have an emotional reaction to something, especially if it is scary or hurtful. But, it is also normal to have a reaction that feels irrational or illogical. Sometimes the programming in our brains causes us to have knee-jerk reactions. It isn't because there is something wrong with us. It is because the brain is trying to protect us.

It's so important to remember that you are normal. It's also important to remember that all emotions and thoughts eventually pass.

The reason this is so important is because if you resist it—if you judge yourself for your thoughts and emotions, if you push against them and add another layer of negative thoughts and emotions on top of it, you only make it worse.

Instead of judging your thoughts or emotions, simply observe them. Notice them. Allow them to be there. Be curious about it, rather than judging. Be gentle with yourself. Then, because you've let go of resistance for a moment, you may find yourself beginning to think more clearly. In that moment, you can remind yourself that you're normal. Everything is okay. This too shall pass.

It's also important to remember that the entire point of learning about all of this is so that you can develop your ability to control it more of the time.

Instead of beating yourself up for your negative thoughts and emotions, celebrate every time you notice that it's happening. Celebrate that although you don't feel in control, you are committed to learning more about your mind and practicing techniques that will help you continue to get better and better at it. You will never be perfect. You'll always have negative thoughts and emotions. But, you'll learn how to not take them so personally or seriously. You'll be able to find clarity and peace, even in the most challenging moments. One day you'll be looking back and thinking, "wow, this would have made me freak out in the past, but now I know I have a choice how I react."

You can do this! You just need to be patient with yourself and accept that you were gifted with a wonderful, powerful machine called the human mind. It's quirky and can get it's wires crossed, but now you have the manual and you can continue to reprogram it so that you can use it to reprogram your life.

8: MINDFULNESS MEDITATION

The term "meditation" often conjures up images of sitting cross-legged on the floor, surrounded by crystals, in a dimly lit room that smells like incense. For some people, this sounds appealing and for others, they assume meditation is a weird, woo-woo, airy fairy experience. But, the truth is that meditation is simply a process of observing and quieting your mind. If you don't like the word meditation, call it focusing.

Mindfulness Meditation

This CBT exercise helps people disengage from obsessive thinking, which means thoughts that have a lot of momentum, by paying attention to the present moment. There has been a significant amount of research conducted on this form of meditation and the positive effects it has on a number of psychological problems.

Simple mindfulness meditation practice:
- Find a quiet place, free of distractions. Your mind will be distracting enough, so make sure you won't be interrupted.
- Sit comfortably in any position you desire. Upright is ideal, however you can lay down if you want to. Just make sure your position is comfortable and will not distract you.
- Start by bringing your attention to your breathing. Notice the sensation of your breath entering and exiting your nose or mouth. Notice how it feels as the air brushes through. Is it cool? Does it tingle?
- Notice the rise and fall of your chest or abdomen as the air fills and then empties your lungs. Do not force or control your breathing, simply allow it to be natural and continue to observe it.
- Watch your breathing for about 5 minutes. During this time, you

will find that your mind will wander of and think about all sorts of things: physical sensations, things you need to do, what happened yesterday. This is totally normal. When you notice your mind has wondered off, simply start noticing your breathing again. You may need to bring it back again and again, and this is wonderful because it means you are becoming mindful!

- The more you practice this, the less your mind will wander. Then, you'll notice you are better able to keep your focus at other times throughout the day as well!
- When you are finished with your 5 minutes, you may notice an increased sense of calm.
- As you get used to this activity, you can increase the time sitting to 10, 15, or 20 minutes. What is most important is consistency, so regardless of how long you sit in this mindful state, do it every day.
- The most important part of developing a daily meditation practice is making it consistent. 5 minutes daily is better than 1 hour once a week.

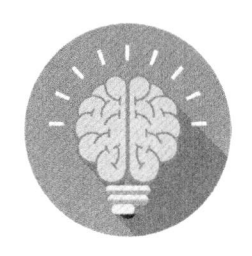

SECTION 5: IRRATIONAL BELIEFS AND EMOTIONAL DISTURBANCES

1: TWO WAYS WE DISTURB OURSELVES EMOTIONALLY

A disturbance is an unhealthy negative emotional reaction to a situation that is caused by an irrational belief. Our goal is to use REBT principles and processes to change the underlying beliefs that cause the disturbances. There are a number of different core beliefs that people can hold that will disturb themselves emotionally, but they fall into 2 general categories.

First, people can hold irrational beliefs about THEMSELVES, or what is often referred to as their ego. These beliefs often are also tied to beliefs about approval by others. This is called an Ego Disturbance.

Second, people can hold irrational beliefs about their emotional or physical COMFORT. This is called a Discomfort Disturbance.

Most people tend to hold irrational beliefs in one of these categories more than the other.

Let's look deeper at what this means.

1. Ego Disturbances are caused by placing unreasonable demands on ourselves, and when we don't meet those demands it impacts our self-image. For example, we may demand that we do well at something and that we must not fail, and we may also tie our need to do well to a need to be approved of by others. If we do not do well, we then feel shameful about our lack of competence and embarrassed due to the perceived scorn of disapproving others. The fear of not doing well and the resulting shame may lead us to avoid any situation in which we might fail or be disapproved of. This in turn may hold us back from what we want to do in life.

2. Discomfort disturbances are caused by placing unreasonable demands on others and on outside situations. For example, we may believe that other people should treat us a certain way. We also may put demands on our environment and the circumstances that we live under. When these demands are unreasonable and our expectations are not met, we feel frustrated or uncomfortable. This disturbance causes harmful emotions and behaviors that would not exist, even in the same circumstances, if the irrational belief was not setting unreasonable expectations in the first place.

Discomfort disturbances comes in two forms: low frustration tolerance and low discomfort tolerance. The two types are similar, and many times are associated or referred to as one and the same. Let's look at both more closely.

2.a. Low frustration tolerance happens when you demand that frustration must not happen in your life. This could be a belief that the world is supposed to make you happy or a belief that everything is supposed to be perfect or ideal. The problem occurs when life inevitably does not make you happy or isn't perfect because you will find the resulting frustration unbearable. You believe it shouldn't be happening. Instead of a minor frustration, it feels horrible.

You may also believe that things have to be the way that you want them to be. But then, when everything isn't exactly as you think it should be, you can't stand it and you make it more significant than it really is or needs to be. Your unrealistic expectation that everything is supposed to go your way makes it challenging to enjoy your world because you're always disappointed.

2.b. Low discomfort-tolerance on the other hand is when you believe that you should not experience emotional or physical discomfort or pain. Then when you experience any physical or emotional discomfort, you catastrophize it and make a big deal about it, like it's the end of the world. Then you don't just experience the pain or sadness, you find the experience absolutely intolerable! And so you are likely to avoid anything that may create any physical or emotional discomfort.

There are a variety of ways that low discomfort-tolerance can negatively impact our lives.

- **Discomfort anxiety:** This is when we experience emotional tension when we feel that our comfort is threatened in any way.
- **Unnecessary worrying:** This is when we worry that the undesired situation may happen, and we dread it because we don't feel like we could stand it. We feel that we must worry about it just in case it happens.
- **Avoidance:** We may avoid experiences, events, or people that may create discomfort that we feel may be too hard to deal with or overcome.
- **Secondary disturbance:** This is when our disturbance creates a second disturbance. For example, we may feel anxious because we are worried that we may feel anxious. You can also be afraid of feeling fear. You can also feel angry at yourself for the behaviors that resulted from your anxiety. In each case you're adding another layer of negative emotion on top of the one you believe you should be experiencing.
- **Quick fix**: In order to cope with undesirable disturbances we may seek instant gratification or short-term pleasure, such as drugs or alcohol or even going on social media for a quick fix of approval.
- **Procrastination:** In this situation we put off doing something because we are avoiding a possible unpleasant situation or not wanting to deal with something that may be difficult or uncomfortable.
- **Negativity and complaining:** This is where we make a big deal about small setbacks, focus our attention on the negative aspects of a situation, ignoring the positive aspects, or compare the situation to other circumstances to highlight what's wrong with the situation, and then of course complain about it to others.

As you can, it's important to understand how our beliefs lead to emotional disturbances, aka undesirable, unhealthy stress, anxiety, anger and sadness. On top of our core beliefs we add another layer of disturbance when we judge situations and assign meaning. That's what we're going to talk about next. Then we'll look at the 3 core beliefs that cause the majority of people's emotional pain, all of which are based on demands we put on our self, others, and the world.

2: EVALUATIVE THINKING: 4 DYSFUNCTIONAL WAYS WE ASSIGN MEANING

In the next chapters we're going to look more closely at the 3 core beliefs that result all irrational thinking. These beliefs are ultimately what cause our emotional disturbances. However, in order to develop an understanding of these beliefs and why they are problematic, we need to look at the evaluative level of thinking. You'll recall that there are 3 levels of thinking: inference, which is when we decide what is going on, evaluation, which is when we decide what it means, and core beliefs, which are the underlying rules that dictate our inference and evaluation.

In REBT we look closely at the way that we evaluate what is going on around us because this is where we have the greatest power to change our thinking. You see, our beliefs are general and we don't put them to use until something happens and we can apply our rules to the situation and evaluate if they're being met. So, once individual situations happen in life, we evaluate what happens and decide what it means.

If you ask yourself or someone else "what does this mean" or "why does this matter" you'll easily get an answer. But, if you immediately asked, "what is the belief that is causing you to have this emotion or think this way?" you would receive only a blank stare.

And, so, in the next section we will begin to look at the process for identifying irrational thinking and rooting out the underlying beliefs, and much of the work will be done at the evaluation level of thinking.

The reason it is so important to understand the way we tend to evaluate what happens in our lives is because the meaning we assign to situations is what ultimately causes our emotional and behavioral response to it. A situation may cause a result in our life at a practical level, but how we think and feel about it is what determines how we experience that result. We've mentioned the idea of a secondary disturbance before, which is when we experience a situation that is already unpleasant or challenging and we add another layer of disturbance by judging the situation in a way that upsets us. You can find yourself in a situation in which you already feel upset because things aren't going your way, and then you can make it worse by evaluating the situation and making a judgment that things are never going to go your way, which of course makes the experience worse.

Irrational Beliefs and Emotional Disturbances

There are 4 main destructive ways that we evaluate life circumstances, including:

1. Demanding
2. Awfulizing
3. People-rating
4. Discomfort intolerance

Demandingness:

The first one, demandingness, is actually the first step to evaluating what something means to us. The other evaluative processes build upon this one. Remember, when we talked about the rules or beliefs we create in attempt at meeting our needs, it isn't the core human needs that cause the problem, it is the demands we put on ourselves, others, and the world regarding what we belief is required for our needs to be met. It's reasonable to need love and belonging and to feel safe, but it's not reasonable to demand approval and unending comfort.

When a situation occurs, we evaluate it and ask ourselves "is this situation meeting my demands and expectations about myself, others, or the world?" Because the belief we hold tells us that these demands MUST be met, if the answer to the question is NO, it causes an emotional disturbance and leads to destructive behavior.

The two words to be on the lookout to spot a demanding belief or evaluation are the words "should" and "must".

The SOLUTION to demanding thinking is to turn the MUST into a PREFERENCE. Tell yourself, "I prefer it to be this way, but if it is not, that's okay too."

Awfulizing:

When a situation occurs, we evaluate it and ask ourselves "how bad is this?" And usually, because our demands aren't being met, our answer is that it's the worst-case scenario, it's horrible, it's awful. We may even ask ourselves "how likely is it to continue to happen or that there will be a terrible consequence?" And, of course, we're likely to think the answer is FOREVER and YES, and so we make it even worse. For example, if your boss tells you that he wants to meet with you, you may evaluate what it means and conclude that it must be something horrible—in fact, you're probably going to be fired. This will impact how you approach the meeting, your emotional state, your interactions with others and every other aspect of your life until you have that meeting. It may turn out that the meeting was to offer you a raise or promotion instead.

The SOLUTION to awfulizing is to remind yourself that it could be worse, it's not the end of the world, and it is temporary. Tell yourself "It's not the end of the world, this too shall pass."

People-rating:

When you or another person display a trait, behavior, or action that does not meet your demands, we evaluate them (or ourselves) and ask "what does this mean about them?" We look at the trait, behavior, or action and judge it as bad because it didn't meet our demand. But then we take it a step further and judge the person as bad too, as unworthy. We equate that one characteristic with the whole person, which ultimately puts ourselves and everyone we observe in a situation in which we have to be perfect in all areas in order to be deemed worthy. One flaw and we're judged as all bad.

This need to rate and judge ourselves leads to low self-confidence, defensiveness, and approval seeking behavior. The need to rate and judge others leads to feelings of superiority, mistreatment of others, and discrimination.

The SOLUTION to people-rating is to recognize that one trait or behavior does not define a person. Tell yourself "All people have both good and bad qualities and everyone is capable of changing and improving."

Discomfort intolerance:

We already talked at length about discomfort intolerance and the emotional disturbance caused by believing that one should never be uncomfortable and should always be perfect and approved of. When a situation occurs we evaluate it by asking "can I stand or tolerate this situation?" And because it doesn't meet our demands the answer is NO. The more uncomfortable it makes us, the more we will do whatever we can to avoid it, eliminate it, or avoid any other similar discomfort.

The SOLUTION to discomfort intolerance is to remember that perfection is impossible and that discomfort is a natural part of life. Tell yourself "I'm not perfect and neither is anyone else. We are all a work in progress. I might not like being uncomfortable, but sometimes the best things in life require stepping out of my comfort zone."

3: THE 6 HUMAN NEEDS

At the core, our decisions and behaviors are driven by underlying needs and our beliefs about how these needs must be met. The 6 human needs are a powerful psychological framework, created by therapist Cloé Madanes and popularized by Anthony Robbins' strategic intervention strategies. These core needs are at the root of our motivations and why we prioritize certain decisions and actions, often without our awareness. Each person values one or more of these needs more than the others. Which need is your primary driver is a huge determining factor for how you live your life.

The 6 human needs are:
1. Certainty/comfort
2. Uncertainty/variety
3. Significance
4. Love and connection
5. Growth
6. Contribution

The first four needs are called the needs of the personality. These four needs are things that we always find ways to meet them—they are vital. The last two are called the needs of the spirit and are needs not always met. In most cases, the first four needs must be met before a person is able to start to value and focus on meeting the last 2 needs. However, when we meet those higher-level needs is when we truly feel fulfilled. Now let's look at each of them.

Need 1: Certainty/Comfort

At our core we want to feel that we are in control of our reality. This feeling gives us security. This allows us to feel comfortable in our life to feel that we can avoid pain and create pleasure. At the core this is just a survival mechanism that we have. Certainty makes us feel safe, emotionally, psychologically, and physically. Depending on how much we value certainty will depend how much risk we take in life. You probably have met people on both ends of the spectrum—those who want to control every single detail in their life and those that crave uncertainty. The extreme need for certainty, however, will hold you back because all growth and change requires uncertainty.

Need 2: Uncertainty/Variety

The second one is uncertainty. Yes, it's the opposite of the first one. Think about it—what would happen if you always knew everything that would happen to you? You would probably be bored to death. So, uncertainty brings excitement and spice to life. The level of uncertainty that you are willing and able to live with determines how much and how fast you will change. Keep in mind that being able to deal with uncertainty is also a skill that can be developed, as you become more confident that you can deal with change. Also, as you start associating uncertainty and change with something that create happiness and helps you achieve your dreams, your desire for uncertainty will increase.

Need 3: Significance

Think about it, we all want to feel like we are special. We want to feel like we are important, needed and unique. There are a variety of ways that we can get significance. For example, you can get it by feeling like you are the best at something, by making a lot of money, having the best house in your neighborhood, by buying the latest thing, getting a master's degree or a doctorate, by becoming a social influencer, by being the best dad, having a bunch of tattoos, you can even be that person that has more problems that anyone else, the most intimidating, or even the most spiritual person. As you can see that there are endless ways to feel significant. People will go to great lengths to feel significant in their life.

Need 4: Love & Connection

The next need is Love and Connection. Whether we realize it or not, love is that thing that we need more than anything. When we love 100% we feel alive and it is a powerful force. For love, many people are willing to do extraordinary things for others, whether it's the love that a parent has for a child or the love of a romantic relationship. However, if we don't feel like we can get love, we settle for connection—even if these connections do not serve us. There are a lot of ways to get connection, whether it is through a friendship, a pet or even connecting to nature. Less-constructive ways of getting connection are through social media, sacrificing our authenticity to conform to a group, or people pleasing.

Need 5: Growth

The next one is the need for growth. Think about it if you're not growing in an area of your life, then that area is dying. This can be your relationship, your business, or an aspect of your personal life. If you are not growing than it does not matter what you are creating in your exterior world. That need for certainty can hold you back from growth, leading you to feel empty and not be able to feel true fulfillment. Growth can be scary because it can have uncertainty for some, but it brings fulfillment.

Need 6: Contribution

The last one is contribution and its one that many people reflect on in the later stages of life, as we look at our legacy. Contribution is like a higher level of the need for significance, the difference being that it's no longer about you. However, contribution is the essence of life. Life is not about me… it's about us. We are social creatures and we have a natural need to feel that we have a higher purpose and that our life has meaning. The way we find that is to contribute to others. In fact, the feeling that we are contributing to others can helps us overcome the biggest changes if we think it has a purpose. Life therefore is about creating meaning, and that comes from giving.

We each have a stronger need for some areas over others at different points in our lives. All of these beliefs are healthy, however we cause ourselves pain when we develop irrational ideas about what we think we need in order to fulfill these core needs.

We need security, but we tell ourselves we need to be free of all discomfort and inconvenience at all times.

We need love, but we tell ourselves we need to be approved of by everyone, at all times.

And, we develop emotional disturbances because of our irrational rules we create about meeting our needs.

So, which need a person values most, and which ones they are starving to meet, will influence the choices that they make in life. They will find a way to meet those needs one way or another, whether through a negative or positive way. For example, someone robbing someone can feel significant, have that thrill of uncertainty, and at the same time they feel certain because they are the one in control. So, this negative action can meet 3 core needs.

The power of identifying your own hierarchy of needs (which one/s are most important to you) is that you can then reflect to see if you're meeting your needs in constructive ways. (And, if not, consciously choose more constructive ways of meeting your needs.)

At the end of the day, fulfillment comes from something internal—whether, deep inside you feel loved, feel like you are growing, and contributing to others. This is why the higher level needs (further down the list) are what ultimately lead to fulfillment. However, in most cases, the lower level needs HAVE to be met in order for a person to turn their attention to the higher level needs.

Let's look at constructive ways of meeting these needs:

- **Certainty:** You can have certainty by having a daily routine or having a community around you that is supportive no matter what's happening in your life.
- **Variety:** You can have variety by adding diverse experiences to your life. You can also try new things and learn new skills.
- **Significance:** You can meet the need of significance by using your talents and skills. You can also master a skill and share your skills with others.
- **Love/Connection:** You can meet this need by establishing life-long friendships spending more time with likeminded people, as well as improving your relationship skills.
- **Growth:** You can meet the need for growth by constantly learning. For example, reading new books, watching YouTube videos, or following others that help you grow. You can also surround yourself with people that motivate you and challenge you to become a better person.
- **Contribution:** You can meet the need of contribution by sharing your talents and passions with others. You can also engage in causes that are meaningful to you.

So, ask yourself:
- Which needs are the most important to you?
- How do you currently meet these needs?
- Which area of need are you currently struggling with the most?
- In what way do you feel like your need is not being met?
- What do you believe is necessary for your need to be met?
- How can you meet these needs in a way that will help you truly be fulfilled?

4: CORE BELIEFS (RULES AND MUSTS) THAT MAKE US MISERABLE

You have probably gathered by this point in the book that it is not the situations in our life that make us miserable, it is the way we think about the situations that determines how we feel. So, why do we assign meaning to life events in the way that we do? The full answer is complex and could fill the pages of another book. The short, yet profound, answer is that all of our pain and suffering is caused by 3 core irrational beliefs.

Not all people hold the same variation of these beliefs, but we all believe them in one situation or another and these beliefs are always irrational. These beliefs are like internal rules that we have for how we, others, and the world "should" behave. The problem is that we normally are not aware that we have these beliefs. And if we do catch ourselves thinking these things, we don't normally question them.

By identifying which of these core irrational beliefs you tend to fall into the most, you can begin to become aware of the situations in which you apply these bogus rules. You can look out for these beliefs in the stories you tell about yourself, others, and your life throughout this book, as well as notice yourself thinking this way in your every day experience. Below you will find a description of the 3 beliefs, as well as additional detail that will help you identify if this belief is active within you. We'll also address the emotional and behavioral consequences for continuing to hold onto these irrational beliefs, as well as present an alternative belief to practice when you catch yourself reverting back to these old, irrational rules.

5: MAJOR MUST #1: APPROVAL—I MUST BE APPROVED OF BY OTHERS TO BE WORTHY.

Need: acceptance, belonging

Fear: judgment, rejection

Demands: I expect myself to perform well and win approval from all significant others at all times, and if not I am a failure, unworthy, and deserve to suffer.

Symptoms:
- Places unrealistic expectations on oneself

- Over-concern with what other people think
- Achievement and popularity determine self-worth
- Self-critical, lack of self-acceptance

Emotional Consequences
- Depression, feeling not good enough, unable to express or embrace true self
- Anxiety, worry about what others think, being judged
- Low confidence, feeling bad about yourself, others disapproval means we are bad, can't be yourself

Behavioral Consequences
- Risk-avoidance, for fear of being judged for failing or being different
- Shyness, for fear of being embarrassed
- Procrastination, for fear of failure, judgment, risk
- Unassertiveness, for fear of rejection or criticism
- Workaholism, in order to gain approval

REPLACE WITH THIS RATIONAL BELIEF:

I have value as a human being simply by being my authentic self, and I desire love only from those who appreciate me and recognize the good in me.

False Sub-Belief:

I need love and approval from EVERYBODY.

Consequence: Stifling of true self, lack of self-love and self-respect.

Truth:
- What matters most is self-acceptance, authenticity, and unconditional love from only the most significant others.
- Everyone has different tastes and preferences and it is impossible to be loved by everybody.
- By doing what others want or expect in order to gain approval,

you are giving away your power to choose how you want to live your life.
- Trying too hard to be approved of has the opposite effect and others will not respect you.
- It may not be pleasant when other people do not like you, but the truth is that it isn't fatal and it doesn't really make a real difference in your life.

False Sub-Belief:

I must be successful, intelligent and competent in all areas.

Consequence: Preoccupation with proving adequacy, even it if means looking competent when you're not.

Truth:
- It is totally natural to be better at some things than others. It is okay to not be good at something.
- You can improve any ability (including intelligence) if you put effort into improving.
- Being afraid of being bad at something you hold you back from trying new things that you're not already good at.
- Failure is a necessary part of growth and improvement.
- Focusing too much on being successful in order to impress others means you are taking time and energy away from things you may care more about.

False Sub-Belief:

I must be dependent on other people because they are stronger than I am, and I can't depend on myself.

Consequence: Leads to unhealthy relationships that burden others and creates attachment based on need rather than genuine love. Doing only what you need help to do actually limits your potential because in most cases your need to depend on others actually holds you back from doing more.

Truth:
- It is true that we all need others to help us learn and to support us during challenging situations, however support from others is

- meant to be temporary and only as needed, with the goal of helping us get to a place where we are caring for ourselves.
- Many people are perfectly capable of doing things on their own but they continue to tell themselves they need others to help them because they are afraid to let go of control of the other person.
- The more you continue to allow others to do things for you the less skill you will develop and the lower your confidence will be.
- If you depend on others to feel safe and confident, there will inevitably be a time they cannot be there for you, which actually makes you less safe and confident than you would be if you relied on yourself.

False Sub-Belief:

My past has made me who I am and will continue to define my future.

Consequence: Continuing to live patterns that do not serve you and failure to reach your potential due to unwillingness to take responsibility for your life.

Truth:
- When you were younger, you did not understand what was happening, and therefore it impacted your behavior automatically. However, now you have the ability to think about your past and present differently and choose to act differently.
- When you were a child, you had no control over what happened in your life, however as an adult you do have control over the decisions you make.
- The past is simply a memory in your mind and has absolutely no way of literally influencing your future. If you are continuing to experience situations that existed in your past that you do not want, you have the option to change them.
- It is true that your past experiences influenced your belief systems, behaviors, and situations you experience in your life today, but now that you know you have a choice all of those things can be changed going forward.

6: MAJOR MUST #2: JUDGMENT—OTHER PEOPLE MUST DO "THE RIGHT THING" AND MEET MY EXPECTATIONS IN ORDER TO BE WORTHY.

Need: importance, superiority

Fear: unfairness, disappointment

Demands: expect all significant others to treat you kindly and fairly, as well as act appropriately, and if they don't they are unworthy, rotten people who deserve to be punished

Symptoms:
- Unrealistic expectations on others, including expecting them to be infallible, perfect
- Assuming you are the sole authority on what is right and wrong
- Assuming you have authority over others
- Believing everyone else is responsible for catering to your needs

Emotional Consequences
- Anger, rage or fury when others intentionally or unintentionally treat you poorly or unfairly or don't meet your expectations
- Impatience with others who make mistakes or aren't perfect
- Bitterness against others for not meeting your needs
- Resentment toward others for being imperfect and especially for treating you unfairly or not meeting your needs

Behavioral Consequences
- Aggression and violence as a way of punishing others for being inappropriate or not meeting expectations
- Bigotry and intolerance of anyone who does not meet your definition of right and wrong
- Bullying others to enforce your belief of the way others should behave or be
- Nagging others to elicit the right action you expect and require

---

REPLACE WITH THIS RATIONAL BELIEF:

All people, including myself, are imperfect, have value to offer, and have a unique perspective of the world.

False Sub-Belief:

I should be concerned and upset about other people's problems.

Consequence: Wasted energy while focused on other people's problems rather than focusing on directing your own life.

Truth:

- Other people's problems almost never have anything to do with you.
- Getting upset because someone else is upset or has a problem does not help them feel better or fix their problem.
- Upsetting yourself about someone else' problem causes you to experience negative emotions for no good reason.
- You do not have the power to change other people or their problems, and reacting emotionally to their problem lessens your ability to support them if that is your goal.
- Focusing on other people's problems takes away time and energy from improving your own life.

False Sub-Belief:

Everyone should treat each other, and especially me, in a fair, considerate manner or they should be punished.

Consequence: Harsh condemnation of and possible lashing out at anyone who does not treat you the way you want to be treated, which is your definition of fairness.

Truth:

- While it is nice to want everyone to act kindly and, specifically, behave in a way that pleases you, however you do not hold authority over other people and it is not your role to punish people for their behavior.

Irrational Beliefs and Emotional Disturbances

- Not everyone has the same definition of fairness or being considerate, and therefore they may act differently than you would expect, however this does not make them a bad person.
- Punishing someone for how they treat another person is not only not effective in changing their behavior, the person punishing them is often exhibiting a worse behavior than the original offense.

False Sub-Belief:

People must be competent and act wisely and if not they have no value and should be punished.

Consequence: Shaming, criticizing, and rejecting others for mistakes, errors, or undeveloped abilities.

Truth:

- This hyper-judgment of others is what causes the cultural perpetuation of approval seeking behavior.
- Everyone naturally has different levels of ability in different areas, however all people are capable of growing in improving in all areas.
- Usually, a person's ability, or lack thereof, is more of a factor of their life circumstances than natural talent.
- When someone makes a mistake or a decision you deem "unwise" there is always a reason behind it, such as not knowing any better, doing the best they are able to do at the time, or having other influences causing their behavior.
- Even if a person has a low level of competence, they still have innate value and dignity as a human being and are worthy of respect.
- Even if a person makes poor choices it does not mean they are not capable of acting more intelligently in another situation where they have different access to information, options, and experience.

False Sub-Belief:

When other people behave badly it means they are bad and should be punished.

Consequence: When others make mistakes or do things you disapprove of, judging them as bad and punishing them: a) equates the behavior with the person and b) does not lead to any form of improvement or resolution.

Truth:
- Human beings are not perfect and make mistakes.
- A person's behavior in one moment does not define their character or worthiness.
- Everyone has a reason for why they act the way they do.
- Everyone has a different perspective of what is right and wrong.
- Punishing someone for their actions does not address the underlying reason for their actions and therefore does not teach them anything.

7: MAJOR MUST #3: COMFORT—LIFE MUST BE EASY, WITHOUT DISCOMFORT OR INCONVENIENCE.

Need: certainty, comfort, justice

Fear: adversity, uncertainty, discomfort

Demands: expect all external conditions to be pleasant and favorable at all times and when they're not it is awful and unbearable.

Symptoms:
- Unrealistic expectations about life being perfect
- Belief that living a trouble-free life is a birthright
- Lack of belief in your ability cope with adversity
- Complete rejection of all life problems as unacceptable

Emotional Consequences
- Low frustration tolerance
- Self-pity and "poor me" attitude
- Depression, hopelessness
- Discomfort anxiety

Behavioral Consequences
- Procrastination
- Shirking
- Drug and alcohol abuse

- Overindulgence in "feel good" behaviors (e.g., overeating)

REPLACE WITH THIS RATIONAL BELIEF:

It is perfectly natural for life conditions to not be ideal or perfect and it's okay if situations do not exist the way I would prefer because I am capable of finding solutions to problems and making changes that bring me happiness and opportunity regardless of the situations that happen around me.

False Sub-Belief:

Things must go the way I want them to go and I should have control over them.

Consequence: Anger and frustration when things don't go the way you want does not help you change the situation. Expecting everything to be exactly as you want it gives away your power to be happy until everything is perfect, which it won't be, ever.

Truth:
- In most situations outside conditions are almost completely outside of your control.
- It is perfectly natural and inevitable for life situations to be unpredictable, uncertain, and rarely to happen the way you believe they should.
- What you do have control over is what happens internally, such as your thoughts and emotions about a situation.
- It is not the outside world and it's conditions that will make you happy and satisfied with life, it is your internal dialog and the perspective you choose to take of those situations.
- It isn't the bad situations that make you unhappy, it's the belief that they shouldn't happen that make you unhappy.
- When something you don't like happens, you can either change it or you can't. If you can change it, take action. If you can't change it, identify what is or could be good about it, how you

could get around it, or what you can learn.

False Sub-Belief:

If something is or may be dangerous or unpleasant I should continue to worry about it.

Consequence: Unnecessary worry causes anxiety and stress and takes away time and energy from productive solutions or other important aspects of life.

Truth:
- Worrying about something does not, under any circumstance, impact the outcome.
- It is normal to feel concerned or anxious about a potential problem, however catastrophizing about it and telling yourself how awful it will be and continuing to obsess over it is completely unnecessary.
- If potential danger or problems can be dealt with ahead of time, take responsibility to identify when and if action can be taken.
- If nothing can be done about the situation, there is no benefit to upset yourself by continuously thinking about it. Worrying does not prevent it from happening. If it's going to happen anyway, you benefit more from being in a more calm, healthy emotional place between now and then.
- In many cases, worrying about something that may happen can actually increase the likelihood of it happening. For instance, if you are driving and you are worried about getting in a car accident, this will make you nervous and your driving abilities will be impaired, making you more likely for you to make a mistake and cause an accident.

False Sub-Belief:

My unhappiness, sorrow, and disturbance are caused by unpleasant or undesirable situations, and therefore I must avoid these situations.

Consequence: Preoccupation with controlling situations and people, leading to frustration when faced with the fact that this is not possible. Avoidance of anything that could go wrong, which leads to a very limited life.

Truth:
- Your unhappiness and disturbance is caused by judgment of the

undesirable situations, not by the situations themselves.
- You have the ability to choose different ways of thinking about other people or situations that makes you feel better.
- It is okay to feel bad about situations and telling yourself the situations should not be there and that you should not feel bad only ads another layer of feeling bad on top of it.

False Sub-Belief:

It is easier to avoid, rather than face and deal with, life's difficulties, challenges and responsibilities.

Consequence: By avoiding difficulties you avoid the potential positive benefit of facing them, plus in many cases you are only putting off problems that you will need to face later, when they will often be worse.

Truth:
- Putting off responsibilities, such as procrastinating, only makes the task harder and more stressful.
- Almost all worthwhile pursuits, accomplishments, goals, and experiences require some level of challenge or unpleasant activity. Therefore, avoiding difficulty prevents you from ever experiencing the desired outcome.
- The more we do something, the less difficult it becomes. In order to get better at anything we first have to experience it being challenging.
- If we do only what is easy we live a very boring experience, limited only to what we are already comfortable with.
- It is perfectly natural and okay to struggle with challenges and responsibilities and it's okay to feel uncomfortable while you overcome them and improve your abilities.

False Sub-Belief:

I am supposed to just be happy. I do not have control over my emotions.

Consequence: When you are not happy all the time you will either blame yourself for being unworthy or blame the outside for not meeting your expectations and making you happy.

Truth:
- While happiness can spontaneously arise when pleasant situations exist in your life, happiness does not depend on favorable

external conditions.

- While it is perfectly normal and natural to have an automatic emotional response to situations in life, it is not the situation itself that causes the emotion, it is the result of the way you think about and judge the stations that happened.
- Happiness can be experienced even simply at the thought of something pleasant, just like anger can be experienced simply by imagining being mistreated. In both cases, the situation is not actually happening, however the emotion is just as real.
- Therefore, emotions are caused by your thoughts, not by situations.
- Happiness is a choice, and long-term, lasting happiness has been proven to be the result of making choices to a) choose a positive perspective of life situations and b) make choices to live in ways that allow you to express your creativity and passions, as well as contributing to others.

False Sub-Belief:

All problems must have a perfect solution and that solution must be found.

Consequence: Inability to accept the reality of a situation and take action to make improvements because the solution is not perfect. Obsession with making a situation perfect, which often makes it worse.

Truth:

- There is almost never a solution to a problem that leads to a perfect outcome.
- Expecting a solution to be perfect will prevent you from identifying possible options or moving forward with any solution at all.

Use the Core Belief Identification Chart on the following pages to identify what type of belief is at the root of your current problem and refer to the ABCDEF process in the following section.

8. CORE BELIEF IDENTIFICATION CHART

3 Levels of Beliefs

Which category does your belief fall under? Which question are you asking yourself?

INFERENCE	EVALUATION	CORE BELIEFS
(Interpretation or Perspective) **Asking "What is happening?"**	*(Demanding, Awfulizing, People-Rating, Discomfort Intolerance)* **Asking "What does it mean?"**	*(Approval, Judgment, Comfort)* **Asking "How do you believe life should be?"**
What are you assuming? What information might you be missing?	Who are you evaluating? You, someone else, the world? What is your conclusion or judgment?	Who or what is not following your rules or living up to your expectations?
See ABCDEF Step 3 (D) PERSPECTIVE	*See ABCDEF Step 4 (D) MEANING*	*See ABCDEF Step 5 (D) BELIEFS*

Identifying Core Beliefs

Step 1: Identify the problem you are having—the activating event, emotional disturbance, or undesirable consequences.

My Problem (Event, Disturbance, Etc.):

Step 2: Go through the following 3 checklists and check off each situation you are experiencing related to this specific problem. Then, tally up your check marks to see which core belief is at the root of your problem.

CORE BELIEF #1—APPROVAL I must be approved of by others to be worthy.	
SITUATIONS/EXPERIENCES	Check √
Places unrealistic expectations on oneself	
Over-concern with what other people think	
Achievement and popularity determine self-worth	
Self-critical, lack of self-acceptance	
Depression, feeling not good enough, unable to express or embrace true self	
Anxiety, worry about what others think, being judged	
Low confidence, feeling bad about yourself, others disapproval means we are bad, can't be yourself	
Risk-avoidance, for fear of being judged for failing or being different	
Shyness, for fear of being embarrassed	
Procrastination, for fear of failure, judgment, risk	
Unassertiveness, for fear of rejection or criticism	
Workaholism, in order to gain approval	

Total: _____ of 12

On a scale of 1 to 10, how much does the following belief relate to your problem? *I expect myself to perform well and win approval from all significant others at all times, and if not I am a failure, unworthy, and deserve to suffer.*

1 --10

Which of the following sub-beliefs most closely relates to your problem?

1) I need love and approval from EVERYONE.
2) I must be successful, intelligent, and competent in all areas.
3) I must be dependent on other people because they are stronger than I am, and I can't depend on myself.

4) My past has made me who I am and will continue to define my future.

How would you re-word the sub-belief you selected so it captures the belief that is leading to your problem?

CORE BELIEF #2—JUDGMENT	
Other people must do "the right thing" and meet my expectations in order to be worthy.	
SITUATIONS/EXPERIENCES	Check √
Places unrealistic expectations on others, expecting them to be infallible/perfect	
Assuming you are the sole authority on what is right and wrong	
Assuming you have authority over others	
Believing others are responsible for catering to your needs	
Anger, rage, or fury when others, intentionally or unintentionally, treat you poorly or unfairly or don't meet your expectations	
Impatience with others who make mistakes or aren't perfect	
Bitterness against others for not meeting your needs	
Resentment toward others for being imperfect and especially for treating you unfairly or not meeting your needs	
Aggression and/or violence as a way of punishing others for being inappropriate or not meeting expectations	
Bigotry and intolerance of anyone who does not meet your definition of right and wrong	
Bullying others to enforce your belief of the way others should behave or be	
Nagging others to elicit the right action you expect and require	
	Total: _____ of 12

On a scale of 1 to 10, how much does the following belief relate to your problem? *I expect all significant others to treat you kindly and fairly, as well as act appropriately, and if they don't they are unworthy, rotten people who deserve to be punished*

1 --10

Which of the following sub-beliefs most closely relates to your problem?

1) I should be concerned and upset about other people's problems.
2) Everyone should treat each other, and especially me, in a fair, considerate manner or they should be punished.
3) People must be competent and act wisely and if not they have no value and should be punished.
4) When other people behave badly it means they are bad and should be punished.

How would you re-word the sub-belief you selected so it captures the belief that is leading to your problem?

| CORE BELIEF #3—COMFORT ||
| **Life must be easy, without discomfort or inconvenience.** ||
SITUATIONS/EXPERIENCES	Check √
Having unrealistic expectations about life being perfect	
Belief that living a trouble-free life is a birthright	
Lack of belief in your ability to cope with adversity	
Complete rejection of all life problems as unacceptable	
Low frustration tolerance	
Self-pity and "poor me" attitude	
Depression, hopelessness	
Discomfort anxiety	
Procrastination	
Shirking responsibility	
Drug and alcohol abuse	
Overindulgence in "feel good" behaviors (e.g. overeating)	

Total: _____ of 12

Irrational Beliefs and Emotional Disturbances

On a scale of 1 to 10, how much does the following belief relate to your problem? *I expect all external conditions to be pleasant and favorable at all times and when they're not it is awful and unbearable.*

1 --10

Which of the following sub-beliefs most closely relates to your problem?

1) Things must go the way I want them to go and I should have control over them.
2) If something is or may be dangerous or unpleasant I should continue to worry about it.
3) My unhappiness, sorrow, and disturbance are caused by unpleasant or undesirable situations, and therefore I must avoid these situations.
4) It is easier to avoid, rather than face and deal with, life's difficulties, challenges and responsibilities.
5) I am supposed to just be happy. I do not have control over my emotions.
6) All problems must have a perfect solution and that solution must be found.

How would you re-word the sub-belief you selected so it captures the belief that is leading to your problem?

Step 3: Review the "truth" statements that correspond to the sub-belief. You can find these earlier in this section. Then, ask yourself the following questions:

Which of the "truth" statements do I find the most believable and empowering?

How would I re-word any of them to turn them into affirmations I could repeat to myself to re-train my thinking in this area?

Step 4: Below are examples of *rational* versions of the 3 Core Irrational Beliefs:

- **Belief 1:** "I expect myself to perform well and win approval from all significant others at all times, and if not I am a failure, unworthy, and deserve to suffer" could be replaced with, "**I have value as a human being simply by being my authentic self, and I desire love only from those who appreciate me and recognize the good in me.**"

- **Belief 2:** "I expect all significant others to treat me kindly and fairly, as well as act appropriately, and if they don't they are unworthy, rotten people who deserve to be punished" could be replaced with, "**All people, including myself, are imperfect, have value to offer, and have a unique perspective of the world.**"

- **Belief 3:** "I expect all external conditions to be pleasant and favorable at all times and when they're not it is awful and unbearable" could be replaced with, "**It is perfectly natural for life conditions to not be ideal or perfect and it's okay if situations do not exist the way I would prefer because I am capable of finding solutions to problems and making changes that bring me happiness and opportunity regardless of the situations that happen around me.**"

Write a NEW, rational, empowering belief that you wish to replace the irrational belief.

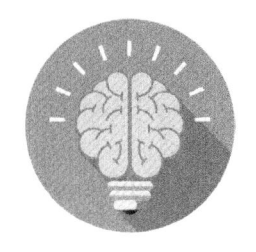

SECTION 6: THE ABCDEF JOURNALING PROCESS

1: WHY JOURNALING IS THE CORE OF CBT AND REBT

Journaling is an essential process for developing a better understanding ourselves and why we do what we do. Journaling helps us investigate and dig deeper, gather data and information, and then reflect.

The processes used in CBT and REBT will uncover thought and behavioral patterns, identify and change irrational beliefs, generate insights into the cause of behaviors, and explore possibilities for creating change. However, the key that unlocks this ability is WRITING EVERYTHING DOWN. Thoughts that aren't recorded cannot be evaluated. Insights that aren't recorded will be forgotten. Changes cannot be made unless they are understood. And this is why journaling is the core process used for CBT and REBT.

This style of journaling is highly focused, meaning what is being written is very specific. Rather than free writing, this journaling focuses specifically on recording thoughts, emotions and behaviors. The goal is to develop awareness of how our thoughts, emotions, and behaviors relate to each other and what causes them, and then to use what is learned to make changes that impact behavior, and therefore, results.

By tracking your experiences, you will begin to see thought patterns, emotional tendencies, and behavior patterns and how they connect. By recording these behaviors and reflecting on what is going on in your mind and your experience, you'll determine which came first, the chicken (the thought) or the egg (the behavior). Actually, you'll find that there is usually a string of cause and effect. Once you can see the patterns, you can change them. You'll be taking mental processes that are happening unconsciously, meaning below your level of awareness, and pulling them into your conscious mind. We'll explore how to develop your awareness of these thoughts and emotions in the developing awareness section.

2: THE ABCDEF JOURNALING PROCESS

All of the different elements of irrational thinking and beliefs that we've learned about can be summed up in one belief: "I am supposed to always get what I want and feel the way I want, and other people and the world must meet these demands."

Deep down what we're really trying to do is keep ourselves safe, be loved, and feel good about ourselves. The underlying drive behind all of this is natural and healthy—but because sometimes our needs aren't met and we don't feel safe or loved or good about ourselves our brains have to try to explain why. We believe that even just the thought that we might not get what we want is cause for concern. The first thing our brain tries to do is to control everything in life. This is where our demanding beliefs come from. The brain believes that if we establish an absolute rule that our needs will be met, we can force life into submission.

But, of course, it doesn't work. When these demands are not met, our brain needs to explain WHY the rules were broken and our needs weren't met. Unfortunately, instead of recognizing that the core belief that everything is supposed to be perfect and under our control is WRONG, it develops new beliefs to explain the problem. These beliefs are usually one of these three things:

1. I am bad or unworthy.
2. They are bad or unworthy.
3. This is the end of the world and I am a victim.

The main premise is that both the underlying rule and the judgment we make when it isn't met are UNTRUE and our demands are NEVER going to be met, and therefore this is the cause of our emotional disturbances.

So, if we can identify and change the core beliefs, we can turn our

The ABCDEF Journaling Process

negative, unhealthy emotional disturbances into healthy emotional reactions that lead to constructive behaviors and desired outcomes. Instead of feeling like other people and the world are blocking us from reaching our goals, we can develop a belief system that helps us stop ourselves from using life circumstances as an excuse to sabotage our own success.

So, how do we do this?

Step 1) First, we identify the PROBLEM by becoming aware of the dysfunctional thinking that's going on.

This has 3 steps:

A. Which stands for ACTIVATING EVENT: Something happens
B. Which stands for BELIEF: You hold a belief about the situation.
C. Which stands for CONSEQUENCE: You have an emotional reaction and a behavioral reaction, which also lead to consequences in our lives.

It is very important to notice that the entire point that CBT and REBT is trying to make is that A does not cause C directly. A situation that happens in life is not what causes us to feel or act a certain way. It is our BELIEF about the situation that causes how we feel and act. However, often it is not obvious what belief is influencing the emotional and behavioral consequences. When working through this process, recognize that often you will need to reflect on the activating event and the emotional and behavioral consequences FIRST in order to then figure out the belief beneath them.

For example:

A. Activating Event: Your employer accuses you of taking money from the register when you didn't.
B. Belief: You believe, "She has no right to do that. She is looking for a reason to fire me!"
C. Consequences: You feel angry and take action based on how you feel, which may be to lash out, putting your job in jeopardy.

In this situation, the lashing out would be a sign that there is a rule being broken, meaning an irrational belief is leading to the unconstructive behavior.

If your belief about the situation was different, your emotional response would have been different:

A. Your employer accuses you of taking money from the register

(even though you didn't).
B. You believe, "I can't lose my job!."
C. You feel anxious and take action based on how you feel, which may be shutting down and being unable to bring up your feelings with your boss.

This belief leads to a different outcome, but it is still actually an irrational belief. It may be true that you don't want to lose your job, but focusing on how terrible it would be causes anxiety which gets in the way of a successful outcome. A rational belief would be to believe "I understand that someone took money from the register and that my boss believes it was me. It is hurtful to think she believes I would do that, but it's just a misunderstanding. I can talk to her about the situation and help her understand that it was not me. I don't want to lose my job, so I want to approach this with care." Of course, you would still feel a little angry, offended, and concerned, but you wouldn't be lashing out or shutting down. You'd be experiencing healthy negative emotions and dealing with the situation with constructive behaviors.

So, the goal of the first step is to identify what is going on and then identify the problem, which is the irrational belief. The reason the belief is the problem is because it is what leads to the undesirable emotions and behaviors that lead to the undesirable negative consequence.

Step 2) Next, we dispute the irrational beliefs—this is step D.

D—Disputing Irrational Thinking. This step includes all 3 levels of irrational thinking.

1. The first part is addressing our inferences or assumptions. Even though when identifying the irrational thinking we said that our inferences were part of the activating event itself, in order to change these assumptions we need to address them separately, which we do at this step in which we're disputing irrational beliefs.
2. The second part is addressing our evaluations and how we assign meaning. While REBT focuses primarily on this part, you will be learning processes for addressing all 3 levels of thinking throughout this book.
3. The third part is addressing the underlying beliefs and changing them to into rational beliefs. This is the ultimate goal of using REBT.

Step 3) Lastly, we create strategies for change.

Now that we have questioned the irrational beliefs and identified the desired rational beliefs, we have two additional steps to take:

Step E—Identify the New Effect we want to experience, which is really identifying the desired consequences, including how we want to feel, behave, and the result we want to experience.

Step F—Identify Further Action that is needed in order to avoid repeating the same irrational thinking or behavior and create lasting change.

So, we have ABCDEF Activating Event, Beliefs, Consequences, Disputing, New Effect, and Further Action. In the next chapters we will explore each step in greater detail, and then in the next sections we will explore processes for changing beliefs by becoming aware of the problem areas, disputing irrational beliefs, and creating strategies for change.

3: SIMPLIFIED ABCDEF FORM

On the next page you will find a simplified ABCDEF form. In the next sections you will learn more about this process, however return here for an easy to use, summarized method for walking through this journaling process. You are also welcome to use a journal to work through this process, or visit the website for this book to download a printable version of this form, as well as other worksheets for other material in this book: https://www.transformationacademy.com/ownersmanual.

A = Activating Event > What's going on?
What is the situation or problem?

- Is it: __real __imagined
- Is it: __past __present __future
- Is it: __external (happening outside of you) __internal (happening inside of you)
- Is it an: __event __experience __person __emotion __thought __behavior __other

Describe the activating event:

What are you experiencing?
- Emotions/Feelings?

    How intense (1 to 10)?
- Physical sensations?

    How intense (1 to 10)?
- If these emotions or sensations happened in the past, during the experience, what are you feeling NOW?

    How intense (1 to 10)?

What are you thinking?
- What automatic thoughts did you about the event while it was happening?

- What did you infer or how did you interpret what was happening?

- What did you assume?

- How much did you believe these thoughts and assumptions while you thought them (1 to 10)?

B = Beliefs > What are your rules?

What are your evaluative beliefs or judgments?

- What does this mean?

- Why is this happening?

- Does it meet my expectations or rules? Which rules does it break?

- What is wrong about this situation? Why is this wrong?

- How do you feel about the fact that this is happening?

- What does it say about you or the people involved?

What TYPE of evaluative beliefs are these?

- Demands (musts and shoulds)
- Awfulizing (catastrophic)
- Discomfort/Frustration Intolerance
- People-rating (of self or others)

What are your core irrational beliefs?

- Which of my rules for how life is supposed to be are being broken?

- Rules about myself and being approved of by others?

- Rules about how other people must behave in order to be worthy?

Rules about how live is supposed to be—meaning if it's meeting my demands for living without discomfort, frustration, or inconvenience. See the Core Belief Identification Chart

C = Consequences > What is your response and what is the resulting outcome?

What unhealthy negative emotions are you experiencing?

- What are the major unhealthy negative emotions that you are experiencing about this event? (Remember, the unhealthy negative emotions are anxiety, depression, guilt, shame, rage, hurt, jealousy, envy)

- How did you feel DURING the event?

- What thoughts were you thinking that lead to this feeling?

- How do you feel now ABOUT this event?

- What thoughts are you thinking now that lead you to feel this way?

- How do you feel about the future consequences of this event?

- What thoughts do you have about how this will impact your future?

What self-defeating or unconstructive behaviors have you done?

- How did you react to the situation? What did you say? Do? Think?

- How have you responded to the situation since it happened up until now? How have you behaved? What did you say or do?

- Have you used any self-protective or over-compensatory behaviors, such as:
    - Gong out of your way to please people
    - Overcompensating to make up for something
    - Pushing yourself too hard
    - Avoiding potentially challenging, uncertain, or unpleasant situations

- Working too hard or trying to prove your worthiness
- Trying too hard to control other people or situations
- Being rebellious in attempt at proving your autonomy
- Other:

What have been the results, outcomes, or repercussions that have happened because of these emotions and behaviors?

- How has how you felt or feel about the situation impacted you? Others (who, specifically)?

- What has happened because of how you felt?

- Can you see how your emotions influenced your behaviors and actions? Which emotions are connected to which behaviors?

- What have been the results or outcomes that occurred because of your actions or behaviors? Which behaviors have resulted in which outcomes?

- What future consequences do you anticipate will happen if you continue with these emotions, actions and behaviors?

- What will happen because of these outcomes?

Have you had any secondary emotional disturbances?
- Looking back at how you felt and acted during the situation, how do you feel ABOUT it?

- Looking at how you have behaved or felt SINCE the experience, or now, how do you feel ABOUT it?

- How do you feel about the results or outcomes that have arisen because of how you felt and acted?

- Imagining the future consequences that you anticipate will result from continuing these thoughts, emotions, and actions, how do you feel ABOUT the future?

D = Disputing > In what ways is your thinking irrational?

Refer to the inferences you identified in step A, specifically the thoughts and assumptions you had about the activating event. Review each inference separately.

- Are they true? How do you know?

- What are you assuming?

- Could you be wrong?

- How else could you interpret this situation?

- What is an alternative way you could think about this? Or, what could you say differently to yourself?

- How much do you believe this new way of thinking?

Refer to the evaluations and judgments you identified in B.

What are you demanding?

- Must it absolutely happen that way or is it possible that it would not?

- What would happen if you didn't get what you wanted?

- What would this look like if you simply preferred it instead of demanded it?

- How would you feel about it?

Are you awfulizing or catastrophizing anything?

How terrible did/does it feel on a scale of 1 to 10?

- If it feels like the worst case scenario, could it actually be worse?

The ABCDEF Journaling Process

- In comparison to other things that are worse, is this really THAT horrible?

- Now that you think about it, how would you ACTUALLY rate how bad this is on a scale of 1 to 10?

Are you avoiding discomfort or frustration because you feel like it's intolerable?

- How terrible did you initially feel like this inconvenience or irritation would be?

- Would it actually be that bad? Would you survive? Is it the end of the world?

- Is it possible that not facing the discomfort or frustration could actually make things WORSE?

- What would be the negative consequences of continuing to avoid it?

Are you people-rating yourself or others?

- Is it possible that the other person (or you) has a reasonable explanation for their behavior? What could it be?

- If the person (or you) made a mistake, is it possible that they will do better next time?

- If the person (or you) is insufficient in a certain area, does this mean they are insufficient in all areas?

- If the person (or you) is flawed in one way, does it mean they are defective or unworthy overall

- If a person (or you) behaves in a way you believe is undesirable or bad, does it automatically mean they are a bad person?

- How would it benefit you and the other party if you accepted that all people are imperfect, yet capable of improvement?

Refer to the musts and core beliefs you identified in B. Again, refer to the Core Belief Identification Chart if needed.
- Which of the 3 major musts applies to your irrational beliefs?
__Approval __Judgment __Comfort

Ask yourself the following questions for EACH of the irrational core beliefs you've identified:
- What is the irrational core belief?

- Why do you believe it? Why does this matter? (For example, you would ask yourself: why must I always get everything right? Why must everyone approve of me? Why does everyone have to love me?)

- What is irrational or illogical about it?

- What evidence can you think of that proves this belief wrong?

- How could you re-write the belief so that it would be based on TRUTH and be rational?

E = New Effect > What is your preferred reaction and desired outcome?

How would you like to experience the ACTIVATING EVENT if it were to happen again?

- Do you expect to be faced with a similar situation again in the future?

- How would you prefer to feel (what are the healthy negative emotions you could shift to)?

- How would you like to interpret the situation next time? How is this different from the first time?

- How would you have to think differently in order to feel the way you want to?

- How would making these changes impact you?

How would you like to change your EVALUATIVE BELIEFS and assign meaning differently?

- How would you prefer to evaluate this situation?

- What would you like to believe that this means?

- What would you need to think or do differently to make this change?

- How would making these changes impact you?

What would you like to believe that is rational that replaces your IRRATIONAL CORE BELIEFS?

- Which specific beliefs are at the core of what's going on here?

- How could you change each of these specific beliefs to be more rational?

- What do you want to believe?

- How would making these changes impact you?

What were or are the emotional consequences of your beliefs?

How would you prefer to feel about the situation?

What were or are the behavioral consequences of your beliefs?

How would you prefer to act or react? How could you behave more constructively?

What is your ultimate goal or desired outcome from changing these beliefs, emotions, and actions?

- What are the negative, undesirable outcomes that have or will result from your feelings or actions?

- What is the outcome or result you would prefer to experience in this current situation?

- What is the outcome or result you would prefer to experience in the future if this situation was ever to happen again?

- What else that you haven't yet identified would you have to change, do, or do differently in order to create this desired outcome?

F = Further Action > What do you need to do next?

Use the space below to identify ideas for activities or processes, whether from this book or elsewhere, as well as additional action steps you are going to take.

Activities or processes from this program I am going to use:

Activity/Process:

Date/Time I will complete them:

Action steps I am going to take:

Action Step:

Goal/Outcome:

Date/Time I will complete them:

The ABCDEF Journaling Process

4: DAILY AND WEEKLY JOURNAL PROMPTS

The following are simplified journal prompts that can be used in addition to or instead of the complete ABCDEF Journaling process.

Journal Prompts for Reflecting on the Day

- What went well today? Can you think of five things?
- What was challenging for you today and what did you learn about yourself from that experience?
- What did you enjoy about today? Can you think of particular experience or examples that made you happy during the day?
- What are you grateful for? Can you think of 10 people or things that you have gratitude for today?
- What do you want to feel tomorrow? What do you desire for yourself tomorrow?

Journal Prompts for Reflecting on the Week

- Who made you feel good this week? What did they do or say?
- What was the biggest mistake you made this week? What did you learn about yourself from this mistake?
- How did you surprise yourself this week? Did you do something the old you would have never been able to do?
- What did you do this week that moved you closer to reaching your goals?
- Is there anything you did this week that you wish you'd done differently?
- What did you enjoy doing this week?
- What did you learn this week?

5: ADDITIONAL JOURNAL PROMPTS

- What makes you unique (positive comments only, please)?
- Write your body a letter thanking it for all it does for you (try not to be negative or body-shaming).
- How do you want to be remembered and what do you need to do in order to be remembered this way?

- Make a list of things you want to do before next year.
- Make a list of your best character traits.
- Make a list of your accomplishments, see if you can go through your life span and list 20.
- What are you really good at?
- How would your best friend describe you?
- What would you do if you knew you could not fail?
- Who are your role models and why? How are you on your path to be more like them?
- What would with your time if money were no object?
- If you could become an expert in any subject or activity, what would it be?
- My favorite way to spend a rainy day is…
- What advice would I have for my teenage self?
- The three moments I will never forget in my life are… (Describe them in detail and why they're so unforgettable.)
- What are 30 things that make you smile? (i.e., kitties)
- My favorite words to live by are…
- I couldn't imagine having to live without…
- When I'm in pain of any kind, the most soothing thing I can do for myself is…
- Make a list of the people in your life who support you and whom you trust. (Then make time to hang out with them.)
- How would you define unconditional love?
- How would you treat yourself if you loved yourself unconditionally? In what ways could you act on these things now?
- If others really knew me they would know that…
- What is enough for you?
- If my body could talk, it would say…
- Think about a way you have supported a friend or relative recently. How you can do the same for yourself.
- What do you love the most about life?
- What always brings tears to your eyes?

- What were your first loves in life, such as favorite people, places or things?
- What 10 empowering words best describe you?
- What has surprised you the most, about yourself, related to your ability to thrive in life?
- What lessons have you learned from your biggest mistakes?
- When do you feel the most energized?
- Make a list of everything that inspires you — including people, books, websites, ideas, art, nature, whatever!
- What's one thing you love to learn more about that would help you live a more fulfilling life? (Great! Now, go study it!)
- When do you feel the most comfortable in your skin?
- Make a list of the things that you've always wanted to say "no" to.
- Make a list of the things you've always wanted to say "yes" to..
- Write yourself a letter telling you what you've always wanted to hear.

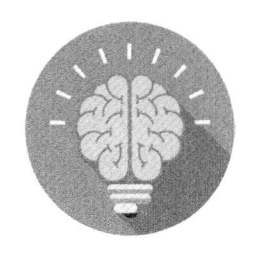

SECTION 7: STEPS 1-3 (A, B & C): IDENTIFYING ACTIVATING EVENTS, BELIEFS & CONSEQUENCES

1: A = ACTIVATING EVENT

We're going to look deeper at the process for each step of the ABCDEF process, starting with A which stands for the Activating Event. Remember to return to the Simplified ABCDEF Form in the previous section to execute the process. You can also download and print worksheets that accompany this book at https://www.transformationacademy.com/ownersmanual. The chapters in this section go along with the ABCDEF activity, and then the rest of the book sections provide additional processes for identifying and changing thoughts and beliefs for each of these steps.

Step 1: Identify the Activating Event:

What is the activating event?

Basically, this means something that is happening that you don't like or that disturbs you. Describe or summarize the situation in a journal or other location where you'll be working through this process. (Note that this process can be used to reflect on an event that happened in the past, however the sooner this process is done after the event happened the more helpful it will be because the details of the experience and thoughts processes going on will be more accurate.)

Step 2: Get More Specific:
- Is it real, such as an event or situation, or imagined, such as a thought or memory?
- Is it past, present, or future?
- Is it external, such as something happening to someone else, or internal, something happen to or inside of you?

Step 3: What Are You Experiencing?
- What are you experiencing, emotionally? How do you feel?

- What physical sensations do you notice (or were you experiencing at the time)?

- How intense are these emotions and sensations on a scale of 1 to 10?

Step 4: What Are You Thinking?
- What are you inferring about the situation? Basically this means what is your interpretation of what is happening?

- What do you assume about it?

One way to identify this is to ask yourself, "what are my automatic

Steps 1-3 (A, B & C) Identifying Activating Events, Beliefs & Consequences

thoughts about this? What is the voice in my head saying?"

How much did you believe in these thoughts and assumptions when you thought them? (On a scale of 1 to 10.)

Let's look at an Example:
- Step 1: Activating Event: Your friend passes you in the street and doesn't say hello.
- Step 2: Specifically, it's a real situation that just happened and you're experiencing it internally.
- Step 3: You're experiencing feeling rejected and sad. There's a tightness in your chest. It's about a 7 on a scale of 1 to 10.
- Step 4: You're thinking to yourself "He is ignoring me. He doesn't like me. I fear I could end up without friends." You believed those first 2 statements at a level 10 and the final one at a level 7.

As you can see, there are multiple things going on in this first step.
- The actual situation
- Your interpretation of it and thoughts about it
- An emotional and physical experience
- Your initial assumptions about the whole experience.

All of this happens in a quick moment and without us being aware that it's happening. To us, it feels like our automatic reaction to what is happening.

In the next step, we'll look a little deeper at the underlying beliefs that cause us to interpret situations the way we do. And then we'll look at the consequences we experience because of our interpretations, assumptions, and beliefs. But, it's important to notice that the activating event itself is not what causes the consequences... the activating event (step A) triggers the beliefs (step B) which lead to the consequences (step C).

Also, another important thing to understand is that these ABC steps can also lead to a loop because the consequences that happen because of the first activating event and belief can become the next activating event that we then respond to based on our beliefs and lead to more consequences.

Once we get to D—Disputing we will be able to break the loop an create change.

2: B = BELIEFS

The second step in the ABCDEF process is B, which stands for the Beliefs. As we discussed earlier, there are two types of beliefs.

First there are the judgments we make about what a situation means (such as demands, awfulizing, discomfort intolerance, and people-rating) and then there are the core irrational beliefs, which we've referred to as demands, musts or rules.

Step 1: Identify Your Evaluative Beliefs:
- What does this mean?

- Why is this happening?

- Does it meet my expectations or rules?

- What is wrong about this situation? Why is this wrong?

- How do you feel about the fact that this is happening?

- What does it say about you or the people involved?

Step 2: Identify the Type of Evaluative Beliefs:
Which category of dysfunctional beliefs do the answers to your questions fall under? By identifying what type of belief is going on, you can more easily identify which activities will help you change the belief.
- Demands, including musts, absolutes and shoulds
- Awfulizing, including worst case scenario, catastrophic thinking, or that it's horrible

Steps 1-3 (A, B & C) Identifying Activating Events, Beliefs & Consequences

- Discomfort intolerance, including feeling like you can't stand being frustrated, uncertain, inconvenienced, or uncomfortable
- People-rating, including judging yourself or others as bad or unworthy

Step 3: Identify Core Irrational Belief (Demands/Musts):

Identifying the core beliefs can take a little digging and contemplation.

Start by asking yourself, which of my rules for how life is supposed to be are being broken:

- Rules about myself and being approved of by others?
- Rules about how other people must behave in order to be worthy?
- Rules about how live is supposed to be—meaning if it's meeting my demands for living without discomfort, frustration, or inconvenience.

For help identifying the core belief or demand, as well as the more specific belief you're struggling with and the truth that will help you shift your belief, see the Core Belief Identification Chart.

RECAP: Let's look at what this would look like using the example from before. So, your friend passed you in the street and didn't say hello. You feel rejected. You assume he doesn't like you and you fear you'll end up with no friends at all.

- Step 1: Now, your evaluative belief or what you believe this means is that "I'm not wanted as a friend, so I must be worthless. It would be terrible to end up without friends."
- Step 2: You're awfulizing and self-rating.
- Step 3: Your core belief that is being triggered is about APPROVAL. You believe that in order to feel worthy I must be approved of by every significant other at all times.

Next, we're going to look at the consequences of your beliefs about this situation. Sometimes you will not be clear about the beliefs until AFTER you identify the consequences. This is because by reflecting on how you feel about a situation and the behaviors you are doing because of the situation you can more easily identify WHY you feel and act that way, which is the core belief. You may need to come back to this step later.

3: C = CONSEQUENCES

The third step in the ABCDEF process is C, which stands for Consequences. Regardless of what happens in life, we always respond in one way or another, whether healthy or unhealthy, positive or negative, taking action or not taking action. In every single case there is a consequence.

In fact, there are four levels consequences:
1. Emotional consequences
2. Behavioral consequences (reactions)
3. Outcomes or results
4. Secondary emotional consequences

It is important to remember here that these consequences are NOT caused by the situations in our lives, they are caused by the thoughts and beliefs we hold ABOUT the situations in our lives. We will continue to come back to this point over and over again until you truly believe that the ENTIRETY of your power lies in your choices for what you THINK, FEEL, and DO.

In fact, all of the consequences we just looked at are because of how you RESPOND to a life situation. This is good news because you are able to CHOOSE how you respond to every situation in life. That is, in fact, where the word responsibility comes from. It literally means "ability to respond". And, so as you continue to work through this process you will be taking responsibility for your thoughts, emotions, and actions, and therefore taking back control of your life.

Congratulations!

Ok, so we already mentioned that sometimes it is helpful to assess the consequences BEFORE we seek to identify and change the underlying core beliefs. There are two reasons for this:

First, sometimes it will be hard to gain clarity about the core belief and looking at how you feel about the situation and how you are responding to it will give you clues to what you would have to BELIEVE in order to be feeling and acting this way.

Second, sometimes looking at the hard truth of the dysfunction and damage your emotions and behaviors are causing to yourself, others, and your life, can be just the wake up call you need to have a strong enough

Steps 1-3 (A, B & C) Identifying Activating Events, Beliefs & Consequences

MOTIVE to commit to changing your thinking.

Motive is, in fact, the root word in MOTIVation for a reason. In order to be motivated to change, you need to have a strong enough reason.

So, let's look at consequences in more detail.

Step 1: Unhealthy Negative Emotions:

- What are the major unhealthy negative emotions that you are experiencing about this event? (Remember, the unhealthy negative emotions are anxiety, depression, guilt, shame, rage, hurt, jealousy, envy)

- How did you feel DURING the event?

- What thoughts were you thinking that lead to this feeling?

- How do you feel now ABOUT this event?

- What thoughts are you thinking now that lead you to feel this way?

- How do you feel about the future consequences of this event?

- What thoughts do you have about how this will impact your future?

Step 2: Self-defeating Behaviors:

1. How did you react to the situation? What did you say? Do? Think?

2. How have you responded to the situation since it happened up until now? How have you behaved? What did you say or do?

3. Have you used any self-protective or over-compensatory behaviors, such as:

    - Gong out of your way to please people
    - Overcompensating to make up for something
    - Pushing yourself too hard
    - Avoiding potentially challenging, uncertain, or unpleasant situations
    - Working too hard or trying to prove your worthiness
    - Trying too hard to control other people or situations
    - Being rebellious in attempt at proving your autonomy

Step 3: Outcomes or Results:

Like we've been trying to point out, the reason that all of this matters is that all of these thoughts, beliefs, emotions, and behaviors lead to real, tangible outcomes or results in our lives. Looking honestly at the repercussions of your actions will help you feel the sting of pain that will help you commit to following through on changing them.

So, ask yourself:

- How has how you felt or feel about the situation impacted you? Others (who, specifically)?

- What has happened because of how you felt?

- Can you see how your emotions influenced your behaviors and actions? Which emotions are connected to which behaviors?

- What have been the results or outcomes that occurred because of your actions or behaviors? Which behaviors have resulted in which outcomes?

- What future consequences do you anticipate will happen if you continue with these emotions, actions and behaviors?

- What will happen because of these outcomes?

Step 4: Secondary Emotional Disturbances

Now that you've identified how your emotions have lead to your actions and how your actions have resulted in the consequences in your life, the next step is to ask yourself how you feel ABOUT these consequences. When we've discussed secondary emotional disturbances previously, we used examples such as feeling guilty about our actions or feeling anxious about our anticipated anxiety. At this stage, we're also going to look at the consequences of these secondary emotions.

So, ask yourself:

- Looking back at how you felt and acted during the situation, how do you feel ABOUT it?

- Looking at how you have behaved or felt SINCE the experience, or now, how do you feel ABOUT it?

- How do you feel about the results or outcomes that have arisen because of how you felt and acted?

- Imagining the future consequences that you anticipate will result from continuing these thoughts, emotions, and actions, how do you feel ABOUT the future?

Once you've identified any problematic unhealthy secondary emotions, you can start this process over again, including going to B to uncover the beliefs that are leading to this secondary emotion.

In fact, you can also look at the negative consequences you have identified here and go back to A, using these consequences as the Activating Event. Again, this ABC process can be never ending loop. However, if you address what is happening NOW, rather than waiting for it to spiral into a greater and greater problem, you can STOP this cycle by moving on to the DISPUTING phase, which is next.

Again, use the activities in the rest of the book to address each of the ABCDEF steps in more detail.

RECAP: Before you move on, let's look at that example we've been using.

Your friend passed you in the street and didn't say hello. You feel rejected. You assume he doesn't like you and you fear you'll end up with no friends at all. Your think this means you're worthless. It feels awful. Your need for approval has been triggered because you believe you must be approved of by everybody at all times.

Now it's time to assess the consequences of this belief.

- Emotional consequence: you feel depressed and worthless
- Behavioral consequence: you avoid people because you believe you're unworthy as a friend
- Result: you become socially isolated
- Secondary emotion: the isolation reinforces the beliefs and increases depression

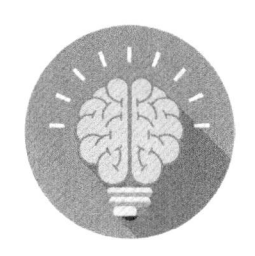

SECTION 8: STEP 4.1 (D): DISPUTING IRRATIONAL THINKING, BELIEFS AND PERSPECTIVES (INFERENCES)

1: D = DISPUTING, PART 1—INFERENCES

The fourth step in the ABCDEF process is D, which stands for Disputing. As we've mentioned, the disputing step is where true change is possible. Until we first identify our thoughts and beliefs and then DISPUTE them we have very little chance of changing how we feel, how we act, or the results we get in our lives.

Like we discussed, the ABC process can get stuck in a loop where our interpretations, emotional reactions, and behaviors continue to cause negative consequences that then become problems themselves. Now that you've evaluated the situation and your perception, emotions, and actions, as well as identified your core beliefs and looked honestly at the consequences of it all, you're ready to dispute those beliefs!

By disputing the beliefs you identified, you break the cycle. However, in order to create true change, you'll need to continue on to steps E and F next.

The good news is that often simply recognizing the beliefs that are at the core of how we feel and act allows us to view them differently because they are quite obviously irrational. However, actually changing the belief permanently or changing how we feel or act in situations takes practice and more extensive re-training of our thoughts.

That's why we address the D step in 4 of the following sections.

First, we'll dispute irrational thinking beliefs in general, by practicing unconditional acceptance, banishing approval-seeking behavior, and using Socratic questioning.

Then, we'll address the 3 levels of thinking, starting with inference. We'll learn how to question our interpretations and assumptions to shift our perspective.

Next, we'll address the second level of thinking—evaluations. We'll use a variety of strategies for changing how we evaluate situations and assign meaning, starting with turning our demands into preferences.

And last, we'll challenging the third level of thinking—our irrational beliefs and learn how to replace them with empowering ones.

But first, let's set a foundation for how to dispute these beliefs. Then, the rest of the activities will build upon this core process.

Step 1: Dispute Your Inferences, Assumptions, and Perspective

Go back and look at what you identified in A. You've already identified the activating event and how you're experiencing it. You should also have identified your initial thoughts or inferences about the situation.

Now, ask yourself the following questions:

- How much did or do you believe these thoughts you held or hold about the situation?

- Are they true?

- What are you assuming?

- Could you be wrong?

Step 4.1 (D) Disputing Irrational Thinking, Beliefs and Perspectives (Inferences)

- How else could you interpret this situation?

- What is an alternative way you could think about this? Or, what could you say differently to yourself?

- How much do you believe this new way of thinking?

RECAP: Looking back at our example about the friend who passed you in the street without acknowledging you, your inference or assumption was that he was ignoring you and doesn't like you. By questioning this interpretation, you realize you may be misinterpreting the situation and that there could be another reason for your friend's behavior.

2: UNCONDITIONAL ACCEPTANCE

The 3 core beliefs we've discussed all stem from a lack of acceptance. Lack of acceptance of:
- Yourself
- Others
- Life circumstances

These beliefs exist because we struggle to accept our reality because our reality does not meet our demands.

Ultimately, the only way to stop these beliefs from continuing to add emotional pain to life circumstances that are already challenging or make minor issues into major disturbances is to counteract the underlying problem. The solution is unconditional acceptance of what IS.

Just like the core beliefs are based on lack of acceptance of three things, the unconditional acceptance must be of all three.
1. Unconditional self-acceptance
2. Unconditional other-acceptance
3. Unconditional life-acceptance

Let's look at each of these forms of acceptance in greater detail.

Unconditional Self-Acceptance

This form of acceptance helps counteract the core belief about approval: I must be approved of by others to be worthy.

The reason people struggle with this is that they put unrealistic expectation on themselves. Then, when they don't meet their own expectations they beat themselves up for it. In order to accept yourself unconditionally, you must practice the following positive self-affirmations:

1. Nobody is perfect, including me. I have flaws just like everyone else, and that's okay.
2. One mistake or failure does not define me. I always have the ability to learn and improve.
3. My past does not define me. I am always able to make decisions for how I will think and behave today and into the future.
4. Being less-than ideal in one area does not define me or define my other traits or abilities.
5. Being perfect or having no flaws would not solve all my problems, make everyone approve of me, or ensure I always get what I want.
6. Having flaws or making mistakes does not make me less worthy than anyone else.
7. Other people's opinions about me are not accurate, because they don't know everything about me, and they do not determine my value or worth. In fact, other people's opinions don't impact me.
8. It is inevitable that not everyone is going to like or approve of me all of the time. It is more important for me to be authentic and approve of myself than it is to try to please others or earn their approval.
9. Although I enjoy being supported by others, I feel even more empowered when I take responsibility for myself and am free to do what I want, regardless of whether others assist me.

Being able to let go of this idea of perfection and truly embracing the perfection in our imperfection can shift many of the irrational thoughts that we have created about ourselves and what we think we should be. It also helps us grow because we can clearly and honestly look at areas that we want to grow, without judging ourselves or being overcritical of the areas that we are working on.

Step 4.1 (D) Disputing Irrational Thinking, Beliefs and Perspectives (Inferences)

Unconditional Other-Acceptance

This form of acceptance helps counteract the core belief about approval: Other people must do "the right thing" and meet my expectations in order to be worthy.

The reason people struggle to accept others is almost always because of the way they perceive that the other person treats them or impacts them. We all want others to treat us a specific way—the way we define as "right". However, the reality is that we cannot control other people, how they act, or how they treat us. People are what they are and by telling ourselves that they're not supposed to be that way, and therefore judging them and being upset that they aren't meeting our demands, only gives us something to be upset about. And, by telling ourselves that we should be able to control other people not only causes ourselves irritation, it also leads us to behave in ways that cause problems with other people.

It is for our own greater good to accept that people are the way they are. This does not mean we have to accept unacceptable behavior or toxic people in our life. What it means is that we have to accept the reality that they ARE that way, whether we think they should be or not. By acknowledging this, we can then choose to disconnect from them or determine how to deal with the reality of the situation.

It is also important to realize that their behavior almost always has nothing to do with us.

Plus, someone's behavior does not define them as a person or determine their worth. For example, someone may react to us in a way we don't want, and so we judge their character. However, their behavior may not have had anything to do with you—they may have had just been having a really bad day. Plus, even if they acted rudely in this one situation, that would not negate all of their positive qualities as a person.

In order to accept others unconditionally, you must practice the following positive self-affirmations:

1. There will always be times that other people treat me unfairly, and even though I want them to treat me fairly, they do not have to do so.
2. Just because someone treats me unfairly does not mean that they are less worthy than anyone else.
3. Everyone has a reason for acting the way they do, even if I don't

approve of their behavior.
4. It is not my job to control other people, however I am in control of my reaction to them.
5. It is no one else's job to meet my needs. I am responsible for taking care of myself, and this is a good thing because it gives me my power back.
6. There will always be people who have a different point of view or belief than me, and that is okay. They have reasons for believing the way the do.
7. If someone's behavior is unacceptable to me, I cannot change it but I can change my interaction with this person.
8. All people are multifaceted, so having a flaw in one area does not mean they are flawed in all areas.
9. All people make mistakes, so one poor choice, behavior, or failure does not mean a person is incapable or unworthy.

Unconditional Life-Acceptance

This form of acceptance helps counteract the core belief about approval: Life must be easy, without discomfort or inconvenience.

Many times, we want to control everything that happens in our environment. However, life is full of surprises. The surprises we don't like we call problems. However, when we accept that life is not perfect and does not unfold the way we always want it to we are open to truly finding the blessings in those unexpected situations. In fact, our biggest challenge can end up being our biggest blessings. However, they can only turn out to be our biggest blessings when we let go of the idea that life must be perfect.

1. Sometimes life's challenges and disappointments can lead to wonderful new possibilities that I never would have known I wanted.
2. No matter what happens in life, I know I am capable of finding a solution and that everything works out in the end.
3. There will inevitably be problems and situations that are outside of my control, however I always have control over my reaction to them.
4. I do not need to worry about potential problems because worrying does not impact the outcome. Instead, I can look for the positive aspects of the situation and seek rational solutions.

Step 4.1 (D) Disputing Irrational Thinking, Beliefs and Perspectives (Inferences)

5. No matter what is happening around me or in the world, I always have a choice what I focus on, how I judge the situation, and how I react to it.
6. Often facing a challenge directly is the best method for finding a solution and feeling better.

3: BANISH APPROVAL-SEEKING AND SAY NO TO "SHOULD"

One of the 3 core beliefs is about the need for approval, and it leads us to judge ourselves and try too hard to gain approval of others. Approval-seeking is one of the most detrimental forces that leads a person to live inauthentically and out of integrity. Instead of making decisions based on what is best for them and instead of honoring who they truly are, they live their life for others—constantly adjusting themselves to be what they believe other people think they SHOULD be.

This approval-seeking behavior is so common that we don't even notice we're doing it. Some people have been people pleasing so long they don't even know who they really are. For me, my approval-seeking behavior started in 5th grade when a boy at my bus stop told me "Natalie, you always act like an animal." The truth is he was probably right. But form that point forward I was always concerned about not looking weird or being judged. Of course, that didn't stop me from being weird because I couldn't help it, and it didn't stop me from being judged… I was made fun of and bullied for many years.

For many people, the approval-seeking behavior starts with their parents. Their parents might be controlling and critical. They may also send mixed messages, for instances telling their child to choose what they want to wear, but then when the child makes their choice, the parent tells them their clothes doesn't match and make them go change. Constantly having their own preferences questioned or criticized leads to a child who, when asked by the store clerk, would you like a lollipop, the child looks at the parent, not because they're looking for the parent to give them permission, but to see if they even want the lollipop at all. They lose their ability to think for themselves. This, unfortunately, follows many people into adulthood.

Common approval-seeking behaviors:
- Changing your opinion at the first sign of disapproval
- Feeling anxious when someone disagrees with you
- Being unable to say "no" and so doing things for people and then resenting them for it.
- Being susceptible to sales people and tending to buy things you don't want
- Apologizing all the time
- Faking knowledge about a topic in order to impress others

If you relate to any of these things, you are not alone! In fact, approval-seeking is one of the most common afflictions! We all want approval and belonging. But, the problem comes when we don't just want people to like us, we demand it. We NEED it. If you simply want approval, you're happy when people like you. But, when you NEED it, you feel like you're going to die if you don't get it. Not only is this a problem because it is inevitable that not everyone is going to like or approve of you… but, it's also a problem because it pushes you away from your true self.

Believing you NEED approval is like saying "your view of me is more important than my own opinion of myself." You sacrifice yourself for the opinions of others.

Think for a moment about a time when you were really upset that someone didn't agree with you or like you or approve of what you did. And now ask yourself, how would your life actually have been different if the person DID approve? In most cases, the truth is it wouldn't have made you any better off.

One of the areas where many people, especially women, tend to become preoccupied about seeking approval from others is how they look. People spend an absurd amount of money and time buying clothes that others view as "name" brand or high-end, cutting and dying and extending their hair, having fake nails installed, filling a closet with shoes, and painting their faces with makeup. Not to mention plastic surgery. When asked, many people say the reason they do it is because it makes them feel better about themselves, more confident. They want to look good. But, what does that really mean? How does having perfectly quaffed hair, eyelash extensions, and $200 shoes actually make you a better person? Why would it make you more confident? You guessed it, because of what you

Step 4.1 (D) Disputing Irrational Thinking, Beliefs and Perspectives (Inferences)

believe OTHER PEOPLE will think about you because of it.

So, the question is, how would other people's approval or envy actually impact you? Does some random stranger looking at you and thinking you look sexy or rich actually mean anything? What would happen if they didn't think you looked great? How would that matter? Actually, if you think about it, in most cases you don't even know if anyone thinks you look great because they don't say anything. And then, when they do say something, often you're annoyed or offended! How much sense does THAT make?

How much energy do you spend wishing you were thinner, more muscular, had better skin, had better hair, had less of a neck glottal, had that new pair of shoes everyone wears these days? Would any of that really matter? And if not, isn't there something else MUCH MORE worthy of your time?

Now don't get me wrong, I think it's a great idea to seek approval of your behavior in the sense that you want to be a kind, considerate person and for people to recognize that. You don't want to denounce approval of others as an excuse to be a jerk and be like "I don't care what you think." But, at the same time, you don't want to be a doormat and bow down to everyone else's desires and demands just so that they think you're nice. Be a good person, but honor yourself first.

The best way to decrease your approval seeking behavior is to practice getting other people out of your head. What I mean by that is to pay attention to the thoughts going on in your head, especially the ones that tell you what you should and shouldn't do.

When you tell yourself you shouldn't do something usually that "should" was told to you by someone else. So, whenever you hear that word "should" it's a sign that you're thinking someone else's thought or believing someone else's belief. The solution is to stop "shoulding" on yourself. Banish the word "should" from your vocabulary. When you hear that voice in your head urging you to do something because you "should", ask yourself:

- Why should I do (or not do) this?
- Who told me I should?
- Do I truly believe I should?

In some cases, it will genuinely be something that you agree you should do 100%. In that case, make it a MUST for yourself and do it!

In most cases you'll recognize that you DON'T really believe you should do it and that you're only trying to make yourself do it because someone else's voice is in your head telling you should. Even if it's not a specific person, in general you are seeking to do what you should in order to gain approval.

It's a bad habit, so be on the lookout for the world SHOULD and question any belief that is attached to it. Then, make your decision based on what YOU truly believe. When you do, you'll be living in integrity with the true you.

4: THE POWER OF PERSPECTIVE

We've already said it multiple times throughout this book… it is not the situations in our life that determine how we feel and the actions we take because of it… it is our PERSPECTIVE of the situation that determines how we feel and behave. What this really means is that if you are feeling terrible or you are doing something that is getting you results you don't want, you need to shift your perspective.

Part of the first step in the ABCDEF process is to identify how you are interpreting the situation or activating event. This usually means what assumptions and judgments are you making about the situation? Once you identify what you are inferring or the perspective you are taking of the situation you can dispute it—meaning you can find another way of looking at and interpreting the situation.

So, what is perspective anyway?

Imagine you're standing on the top of a hill, back to back with your friend. In front of you, at the bottom of the hill, is a collection of dilapidated homes. Their roofs are covered in tattered tarps from leaks that were never fixed. There are heaps of trash along the street, and a group of young children are running together in bare feet kicking a deflated soccer ball. Your heart hurts as you observe the extreme poverty that these children live in. You say to your friend, who is standing behind you facing the other direction, can you believe this? It's so sad!

Your friend responds, what do you mean? This is amazing! You're thinking to yourself, what? How could this be amazing? But then you

Step 4.1 (D) Disputing Irrational Thinking, Beliefs and Perspectives (Inferences)

realize that your friend is looking the other way. Your friend is seeing the world from a different angle or point of view. Your friend has a different perspective. You turn around to get a glimpse of what your friend sees from their perspective and you see a beautiful view of a sunset over a lake. Amazing indeed.

This example shows that every person has a different perspective in life and just because someone else believes something different than you do does not mean they are wrong—they are just seeing the world in a different way.

But, an even more important aspect of perspective is when we INTERPRET the world we see.

This time, imagine you and your friend are standing atop the hill but this time you're both facing the dilapidated houses. Your response is still "can you believe this? It's so sad!" But your friend says to you, "I think it's amazing!" At first you're horrified. How could this be amazing? But then you decide to ask what they mean. Your friend replies, "It's amazing that even in such a terrible environment those kids are able to have fun and experience joy. I find it inspirational"

In this situation, both you and your friend are seeing the same exact circumstances yet your perspectives—or how you interpret the situation—are very different. In this case, you are making a negative inference. Your negative thoughts about the situation make you feel upset about it. Your friend, however, has positive thoughts about the situation and so feels great. The situation is not responsible for how either of you feel—your thoughts about it are responsible.

But, it isn't even just that your thoughts were negative and your friend's thoughts were positive. Another factor that impacts your reaction to the situation is what you are ASSUMING about it. Your friend assumes that the children are happy, while you assume that they are unhappy, or at least you think they should be because, after all, you would be unhappy if you lived in those conditions.

So, this story shows that there are two ways your inferences can become problematic.
1. You can make incorrect assumptions about a situation
2. You can interpret situations in a negative way

First, let's look at assumptions.

No matter what is happening in our life or around us, there is always a limit to what we actually know about what is happening. We can't see what is happening that isn't right in front of us. We don't know what happened previously. We don't know much about the people involved and we definitely don't know what they think or feel. But, our brains love certainty and always seek to form conclusions, and so we make assumptions about the situation. We specifically make assumptions about whether or not we believe the situation or people involved are meeting our expectations and demands.

Whatever we don't know, we fill in the gap. We make up a story to explain what we're seeing or experiencing so we can explain to ourselves what is happening.

Then we believe our conclusion about the situation is fact—that it is reality. But, the truth is that we're almost entirely wrong.

Then, we use this perspective we have about reality to make our next judgment, which is the next step—we determine what we believe all of this MEANS.

All of this assuming and perspective-taking reality all happens automatically and in a split second.

However, once you become aware, either by noticing your emotional reaction, noticing what you're thinking or saying, or noticing the consequence of your point of view—such as how you acted in response—you can choose to reflect on what you were thinking about the situation that caused your reaction to it.

Ask yourself:
- What do I believe is/was going on?

- What assumptions did I make about it?

- Is my perspective true?

- How do I know?

- What do I not know for sure about the situation?

Step 4.1 (D) Disputing Irrational Thinking, Beliefs and Perspectives (Inferences)

- Could someone else have a different perspective of this?

- What other ways could I look at this?

- In what way could I choose to look at this situation in order to see the good, feel more positive about it, or find the silver lining?

This last question is important because the way we interpret a situation determines how we feel about it and how we feel ultimately determines our experience as well as our behavior. If the situation is what it is, which it always is, the first step is to try to interpret it rationally and accurately by recognizing that there is much we do NOT know about it. The second step is to find a way to look at it that focuses on the positive and helps us feel healthy emotions about it. Why does this matter? Because feeling bad about ANYTHING does not make the situation better. If you're going to have to be stuck waiting in line anyway, you might as well enjoy the experience, right? In the same way, if a situation is challenging, you might as well find an optimistic way of looking at it so that you feel hopeful and seek a solution rather than complaining, feeling sorry for yourself, and shutting down.

Choosing your perspective is one of the most powerful superpowers you have, and one you probably have not been using to its full capacity. The other chapters in this section will help you shift your perspective and practice positive thinking.

5: REFRAME NEGATIVE EXPERIENCES

Imagine each situation in life is like a photo in a frame. The frame that holds the photo influences how the photo appears. Other things around the photo also impact how you perceive it, such as the lighting, the color of the wall, or where it's hung. These differences can even change the meaning of the photo. A photo of an explosion that is hanging on the wall in an office building that says "blow up your limits" means something totally different than that exact same photo hanging on a wall in a war memorial museum. With any photo or situation in life, if you change the frame or the way you're looking at it, the meaning changes.

That's why we change our perspective of a situation, we call it "reframing".

The Power of Interpretation or Perspective

You may not always be able to change what happens around you, but you always have a choice of how you respond, react, and how you view the situation. The situation itself does not determine the outcome, your perspective does.

Even the worst experiences of life, that feel like a curse, can be reframed to find the blessing contained within them. It is the MEANING we attach to a situation that determines whether it moves us forward or holds us back.

Practice Finding the Silver Lining

For every seemingly negative circumstance in life, there either was (or could be) a positive outcome because of it.

- If your relationship hadn't ended bitterly, you may not have the loving relationship you have today.
- If you had not been downsized during the recession, you may not have returned to school and changed your career.
- If you had never made mistakes, you never would have learned the lessons that made you who you are today.
- If you had never experienced loss of a loved one, you would not have the same appreciation for those in your life today.

The moral of the story is that you always have a CHOICE of to look for the silver lining in any situation.

Reframe Negative Experiences

When something happens that makes you frustrated, sad, angry, or disappointed, ask yourself the following questions:

- What else might be going on here?

- What did I learn from this experience?

- What can I do differently next time?

Step 4.1 (D) Disputing Irrational Thinking, Beliefs and Perspectives (Inferences)

- What positive outcome eventually came as a result of this situation?

- What meaning does it have? What purpose does it give me?

- How can I use this for GOOD?

Practice: Make a list of any experiences from your past that were "negative" and then identify the positive outcomes and/or the empowering lessons you can take from them.

Change Your Perspective and Your Words

The words you use are one powerful way to shift your perspective. For example, the word "fail" can conjure up strong emotions and fear. To someone with a fixed mindset, failure is the ultimate worst-case scenario because it means you ARE a failure.

By changing your perspective, you can change the way you view failure. Let's try it now.

The truth about failure is that as long as you learn something from it that you apply to your life, nothing is lost. It is only failure if you either don't learn from it and give up or if never try in the first place.

Imagine you wanted to climb a mountain. You're standing at the bottom looking up, feeling afraid that you might fail. But, you are already in the failure position. Why? Well, because if you tried climbing the mountain and failed, you'd end up back where you are. So, not trying to climb the mountain is the same as failing.

There are also many stories of famous failures that illustrate how failure is not a death sentence. Walt Disney was fired from a job and was told he lacked imagination. Steven Spielberg was rejected by the cinematic school he applied to. But, they didn't see their failure as a reflection on themselves, they saw their failure as a learning opportunity.

Using the analogy of the mountain to see that not trying is the same as failure takes the fear out of failure because you realize you have nothing to lose. Finding evidence that supports that failure is not a bad thing helps us remember to look for the silver linings and what can be learned.

Another step you can take is to change the words you use. For instance, next time you hear yourself thinking or saying the world "fail", replace it with "learn". The new word helps you re-frame the situation and remember to look for the lesson.

Here's another example: the next time you catch yourself thinking "I'm not good at this", always add the word "yet". This lets your mind know that although you may not have the ability, this does not mean you can't. By telling your unconscious mind that you can develop the ability, you have given it a command and it immediately starts to tune into finding ways for you to learn and grow. This is the power of your words to change your perspective.

6: POSITIVE THINKING AND AFFIRMATIONS

Positive Thinking

When you're in the midst of having a negative thought and the associated negative emotion it can be really hard to think positively. Even if the negative thought is faulty or untrue, it feels so right and real in the moment.

Positive thinking isn't about fooling yourself, it's about thinking MORE positively than your current negative state. That's why it's important to practice improving your thoughts, gradually. You see, the thought has momentum, like a car rolling down a hill. If you try to jump out in front of it and force yourself to change your thought, it will run you right over.

If you're thoughts are telling you "I'm unworthy", trying to tell yourself "I am powerful and amazing" may sound ridiculous to yourself at the time. It's unbelievable. Instead, you need to slow it down with incrementally better thoughts. Instead of reaching for the best thought ever, just try to reach for something a little better that feels believable to you from where you are. For instance, start with "I matter to a few people" and then "I have done important things in the past" and work your way up to "what I do with my makes a difference to others" and finally to "I matter".

Another way to counteract negative thoughts is to be preemptive. Instead of waiting until you're in the midst of a powerful negative thought to try to change your mind, practice positive thoughts ahead of time. Doing this can reprogram your thoughts and prevent those negative thoughts from happening, and when they do they are less powerful.

This process, often called affirmations, is the most effective when

Step 4.1 (D) Disputing Irrational Thinking, Beliefs and Perspectives (Inferences)

used for negative thoughts that you have regularly.

Affirmations

Affirmations are written or spoken positive statements that, when consistently practiced, rewire our thoughts and beliefs.

If you have a repetitive negative thought that causes you to feel bad, you can replace it with an empowering thought. If you repeat it to yourself regularly, such as when the negative belief is triggered AND at pre-determined times of the day, you practice this new belief, helping it become ingrained into your implicit, automatic, memory. Over time this thought becomes habituated and you BELIEVE it.

After you have created your affirmations, the next time you catch yourself thinking one of those repetitive negative thoughts, you can remind yourself of the new positive thought you've created to replace it. Because it's something you do repeatedly, using this new thought helps slow the momentum of the negative thought much faster than the first method we discussed.

The 4 P's for Successful Affirmation Statements

- Personal (I, Me statements)
- Passion (put emotion into it)
- Present (as if it's already happening, not future)
- Positive (avoid words like "not" or "don't")

Lastly, you must repeat it REGULARLY.

Activity

For this activity you can focus on one thought you are looking to counteract, or you can brainstorm a number of different repetitive thoughts. What NEGATIVE BELIEFS to you commonly think to yourself (or even say out loud) about yourself, your capabilities, your confidence, or anything else that holds you back?

For each negative belief, write a NEW phrase that is positive and empowering, using the guidelines above. Ask yourself, what would counteract the negative thought—nullify it? What would be the opposite? What do you WANT to think or believe in this situation?

Repeat this affirmative statement at least 3 times a day (5 to 10 times each session). Consider posting it on your mirror, computer or nightstand where you can see it regularly.

The next activity uses a similar process to identify the lies we tell ourselves or the negative thoughts we think about ourselves and replace them with the truth!

7: STOP IRRATIONAL AND ILLOGICAL THINKING WITH SOCRATIC QUESTIONING

The truth is that we all think illogically or irrationally sometimes. I'm sure you know people who say things that you really wonder to yourself "how could they possibly think that?" Or, maybe you've had an argument with someone and it feels like you're spinning in circles or that you're talking to a brick wall. This happens because it's easy to get locked into a thinking pattern that doesn't make any sense. But, the truth is that sometimes the person who is stuck in illogical thinking is YOU. Something can make so much sense to us at the time, but then someone points something out or you find our more information later that helps you realize that the way you were thinking about the situation made no sense.

When you're emotional, in fact, almost all thinking is irrational. The reason is that when we become emotional, our emotional center in our brain called the amygdala kicks on and floods our bodies with chemicals. At the same time, the prefrontal cortex, which is responsible for rational thought, shuts off. Our ability to think logically is literally impaired until our emotions are back under control. This is a really good reason for never making decisions when you're highly emotional AND why to never continue to talk or argue when either you or the other person is highly emotional. Nothing good will come out of it.

But sometimes, emotions aside, our thoughts are irrational because there are so many assumptions, distortions, and limited perspectives that can lead us not to be clear with our thinking. The good news is that there are ways to root out illogical thoughts, which is important because if our thoughts impact our emotions and actions we don't want to be creating our life experience based on thoughts that aren't even true.

This is where Socratic questioning comes in, also referred to cognitive restructuring.

Step 4.1 (D) Disputing Irrational Thinking, Beliefs and Perspectives (Inferences)

Socrates is an early Greek philosopher who was one of the greatest thinkers of all time. He was famous for his ability to prove that someone else's thinking was illogical. The person would state their opinion and then Socrates would ask them questions until he led the person to make a statement that contradicted their original claim, showing that their original opinion was illogical.

The philosophy behind this type of questioning is that disciplined questioning can help a person uncover the truth, expand their thinking, uncover assumptions, and follow a line of thought all the way through. You'll notice that this type of questioning is used in a number of activities throughout the program.

Thoughts are going on inside our minds all the time like a running dialog. They happen fast and we often aren't really aware they're happening. We have an entire section dedicated to developing awareness, but to start use this activity to begin tune into your thoughts. Use Socratic questioning on yourself to determine if what you are thinking is logical.

These questions will help you develop a greater understanding of WHY you think what you think and whether the thought is rational and logical. Then, later in the book we'll look at how to use this type of questioning to question underlying belief systems.

Socratic Questions
- What is the thought you would like to question?

- What evidence is there that this thought is accurate?

- What evidence exists that calls it into question?

- Is this evidence based on facts or your feelings?

- Is your thinking black and white or all-or-nothing?

- Is the situation more complex than what you are assuming?

- Could you be misinterpreting the evidence or making any unverified assumptions?

- Would other people have different interpretations of the same situation? If so, what might they think?

- Are you looking at ALL relevant evidence, not looking only at the evidence that supports what you already believe?

- Are you exaggerating or thinking this way just because it's your habit?

- Where did this thought came from? Who may have passed it onto you? Are they a valuable source?

8: PUTTING THOUGHTS ON TRIAL

Pretend as if you are putting your thoughts on trail. You are trying to prove it WRONG. You will you play the defense attorney, the prosecutor and the judge. You will provide evidence for and against the thought, in order to determine if it is based on fact,

- Write down the thought that you want to put on trial.

- The Defender: What evidence will you present to the Judge to support it?

- The Prosecutor: What evidence will you present that calls the other evidence into question?

Step 4.1 (D) Disputing Irrational Thinking, Beliefs and Perspectives (Inferences)

- The Judge: Now that you've seen the evidence from both sides, as an impartial judge, how would you rule in this case?

10: FACT OR OPINION

Thoughts are Not Facts

Most people assume that thoughts are equivalent to facts, but that is rarely true! It takes practice to learn how to identify the difference between opinion and fact. In the activity below, next to each statement decide whether it is a fact or an opinion.

	FACT:	OPINION:
1. "She is a bad person"		
2. "Amanda told me she didn't like what I said in the meeting"		
3. "Nothing ever goes my way"		
4. "This project is going to be a disaster"		
5. "I'm not as good looking as he is"		
6. "I failed the test"		
7. "I am overweight"		
8. "She yelled at me"		
9. "He is selfish"		
10. "There's something wrong with me"		
11. "I'm lazy"		
12. "My friend didn't lend me money when I asked"		
14. "My feet are too big"		
15. "I'm ugly"		
16. "Nobody will ever love me"		

Answers: Facts (2, 6, 7, 8, 12), Opinions (1, 3, 4, 5, 9, 10, 11, 14, 15, 16)

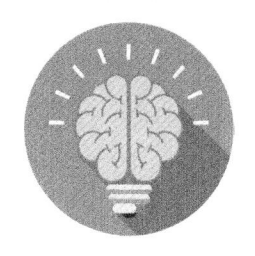

SECTION 9: STEP 4.2 (D): CHANGING THE MEANING YOU ASSIGN (EVALUATIONS)

1: D = DISPUTING, PART 2—EVALUATIONS

Step 2: Dispute Your Evaluations

Go back and look at what you identified about your evaluations in B. You already identified what you believe this situation means and how you feel about it.

Now, ask yourself the following questions:

- What are you demanding?

- Must it absolutely happen that way or is it possible that it would not?
- What would happen if you didn't get what you wanted?

- How would you feel about it if you simply preferred it instead of demanded it?

Are you awfulizing / catastrophizing anything? __Y __N

How terrible did/does it feel on a scale of 1 to 10?

- If it feels like the worst case scenario, could it actually be worse?

- In comparison to other things that are worse, is this really THAT horrible?

- Now that you think about it, how would you ACTUALLY rate how bad this is on a scale of 1 to 10?

Are you avoiding discomfort or frustration because you feel like it's intolerable? __Y __N

- How terrible did you initially feel like this inconvenience or irritation would be?

- Would it actually be that bad? Would you survive? Is it the end of the world?

- Is it possible that not facing the discomfort or frustration could actually make things WORSE?

- What would be the negative consequences of continuing to avoid it?

Are you people-rating yourself or others? __Y __N

- Is it possible that the other person (or you) has a reasonable explanation for their behavior? What could it be?

- If the person (or you) made a mistake, is it possible that they will do better next time?

- If the person (or you) is insufficient in a certain area, does this mean they are insufficient in all areas?

- If the person (or you) is flawed in one way, does it mean they are defective or unworthy overall?

- If a person (or you) behaves in a way you believe is undesirable or bad, does it automatically mean they are a bad person?

- How would it benefit you and the other party if you accepted that all people are imperfect, yet capable of improvement?

Again, looking at our example about the friend who passed you in the street without acknowledging you, your evaluative belief was that you are unacceptable as a friend, you'll never have friends again, and you're unworthy.

When you question this belief, you realize that it can't be true because you do, in fact, have other friends and it is reasonable to believe you will have friends in the future as well.

And, you recognize that even if you did not have friends that does not define the entirety of yourself as a person or determine your worthiness.

2: CHANGING YOUR EVALUATIVE THINKING

So much of what we experience as a reaction to life happens on autopilot, including our initial thoughts, assumptions, emotions, and initial behaviors. It can be challenging to even notice what we are thinking, feeling, or doing in the moment. But, how we evaluate what all of that means is a cognitive process that is a little easier to become aware of. This is why we have said that our EVALUATIONS is the point in this process where we hold the most power to change our thinking. Whether we catch ourselves having a negative reaction to something in the moment or we're reflecting back on it after the fact, once we are aware there is a problem, the MOST IMPORTANT question to ask is—what does this mean?

The goal is to identify how we initially assign meaning and then to question ourselves in order to change the meaning we assign.

Earlier in the book we talked about evaluative thinking and the 4 dysfunctional ways we tend to assign meaning. In this section we're going to look at how to shift how we evaluate what a situation means by turning these dysfunctional ways of thinking upside down.

First, we'll address demandingness by looking at how to turn our demands into preferences.

Then, we'll address our tendency to awfulize and make things appear worse than they are with several activities meant to help you overcome worry.

We'll also look at our tendency to people-rate as well as how to develop a tolerance for feeling uncomfortable and embracing uncertainty.

The activities in this section address different aspects of evaluative thinking and can be used depending on what areas you are struggling with the most.

3: TURNING DEMANDS INTO PREFERENCES

You'll remember that when we talked about what causes emotional disturbances, what was really going on is that we had placed demands on ourselves, others, and the world and because our demands weren't met we evaluated the situation (such as awfulizing) and we had a negative emotional response to it.

Our unreasonable demands, musts, needs or expectations are what cause our emotional disturbances. The solution is to tame our demands so we don't have such an emotionally charged response to them. We need to downgrade our demands to preferences.

If what you prefer doesn't happen, it doesn't feel like the end of the world. But, when your demand or need isn't met, it feels absolutely terrible. By shifting our desires for the way we want things to be to be preferences, not needs, we are better able to cope with not getting our way.

Here is a process for turning demands into preferences:

Step 4.2 (D) Changing the Meaning You Assign (Evaluations)

	My Demanding Belief:	My Alternative Belief (Preference):
Irrational or rational?		
Which is true?		
What is your evidence for why you chose true or false?		
Which is helpful/healthy and which is unhelpful/unhealthy?		
Which is sensible/logical and which is illogical?		
What is your evidence for why you chose logical or illogical?		
Which do you want to strengthen and act on?		
What are your reasons for your choice?		

4: EXPAND YOUR BOUNDARIES AND EMBRACE UNCERTAINTY

Escape from Darkness

When I (Natalie) decided to Florida from New Hampshire when I was 23, everyone I told responded with pessimism and discouragement. "You'll be back." "It's too hot down there, you're going to roast." "There are old people everywhere." "The water at the beach gets so warm it's not even refreshing." "I've heard the traffic is TERRIBLE." Everyone had negative things to say. Everyone except one guy who responded more honestly. When I mentioned I was moving to Florida he paused for a moment, reflectively, and said "I wish I had the balls. I've always thought about moving south to get away from these horrendous winters, but the truth is I'm just too much of a chicken."

I thanked him for his honesty and told him what I had just realized in that moment—that most of the rest of the people I'd told, who had reacted with negativity, had probably also always thought about moving south but that, unlike him, they couldn't face the truth.

The truth is that they avoided acknowledging their desire for a better (or at least warmer) life out of fear.

They limited themselves to avoid the discomfort of change. So, my brazen and abrupt move to the other side of the country—without a job or a house or a nest egg—threatened the tightly held belief they clung to that it wasn't possible. It might have been a little crazy, but it was definitely possible.

After the winter we had just experienced—with practically zero snow and temperatures so cold they close the schools for cold—the only thing I saw as "crazy" was living through another year in a frozen hell.

Hunger for Light

I distinctly remember the moment I made my decision. It was February, and the little snow we had was melting and a patch of brown and crumpled grass was showing through. I saw a small green sprout reaching toward the sun. I empathized with it's hunger for the light. I felt compassion for the months it had spent trapped beneath the frozen earth. I felt the relief of breaking through. I realized it was not the plight of the sprout I

Step 4.2 (D) Changing the Meaning You Assign (Evaluations)

was empathizing with, it was my own.

> *"Never again," I said to myself in that moment. And I meant it. Fear of the unknown or not, I was not about to submit myself to further torture within a self-inflicted boundary of a state.*

I arrived in Florida on April 1st, but I can assure you it was not I who was the fool. 13 years later, I'm still here. I live at the beach. And all of those people's fears were totally bogus, especially the one about the warm water. 88 degree Gulf Beach water is like a saltwater spa. It is heaven. Stop lying to yourself!

Mental Boundaries

So, the other day I was in the Florida Keys celebrating my birthday with my husband and daughter on a snorkeling trip. On my way there, we stopped to visit family, and at our hotel the attendant asked where we were from and what we were there for. When we said we lived 4 hours away and were heading to Key Largo, he mentioned that he'd always wanted to go to the Keys, but that anything over an hour away is too far. From the hotel, Key Largo was little more than 90 minutes south.

> *I thought to myself, "too far for what?" For experiences worth having? For opportunities and beauty and adventure? For life to exist?*

It reminded me of the limited mental boundaries that I once held for myself. You see, after moving to a giant state like Florida I realized that most people in small states develop what I call "small state mentality". For some reason, there seems to be a psychological boundary around the literal boundary of one's home state. For whatever reason, it feels weird to cross it. In Florida, I found myself driving 3 or 4 hours away without questioning it, which I found odd because when I lived in New Hampshire it felt absurd to drive to Boston, which was only an hour away. New York City (2 states away) was only 4 hours away, yet I never would have thought of going. My loss! But, in Florida, you can drive 8 hours and still be in Florida.

This hotel attendant reminded me that it isn't just people who inhabit small states who develop this mental boundary—it's everyone—except other people's boundary is a certain driving distance. It seems so normal for me to drive long distances to experience places I'd like to go that it always surprises me when I meet people who live out their lives within an hour radius. For some, it's a 20 minute radius.

I find it creepy. Even creepier are the people who live within their radius in the same town they grew up in. Eeek. I simply cannot imagine living such a limited life.

Self-Imposed Limitations

These mental physical boundaries are a perfect example of self-inflicted limits. Whether it's a state or a certain distance from home, these boundaries are ultimately meaningless. I challenge you to ask anyone (yourself included) what reason they have for not wanting to go beyond whatever boundary they've set for themselves, and I assure you there will be no reason. What could the reason possibly be? Sitting in a car is too painful? Slight discomfort or boredom are simply too much to bear? Their brain will explode if they drive too far? They have an irrational fear of being chased by rabid baboons? WHAT IS IT?!

The only legitimate reason I can think of is that they fear that they may experience something beyond that boundary that challenges their belief that their life is what they want and that everything they could ever need or love exists within a 20 minute radius

What's your boundary? 20 minutes? 60? 4 hours?

What about with regard to your job? Will you only work somewhere within 20 minutes of your house? It's understandable if you don't want to waste your time commuting, but what if your absolutely ideal dream job was 45 minutes away? Would enjoying what you spend 8 hours a day doing be worth spending an extra hour on the road? Or, what if you are happy with your job but your dream beach house became available at a price you could not refuse. Would it be worth driving an hour each way to spend your time at home listening to the waves lap upon the shore, watching the sunset, and swimming when you want to?

It's a toss up... you have to choose between your *time* and the *quality* of how you spend your time. Or, you can completely re-think the whole thing, like I did, and create your own job and work from home at the beach.

The truth is that you have a choice but that you don't allow yourself the full range of options because you create imaginary boundaries of limitation.

Stop it.

Excuses are Choices

I didn't spend a couple days on vacation in the keys because I have the money and flexibility to do it. I have the money and flexibility to do it because long ago I made a decision to expand my boundaries. At a time when my peers were settling in with their small state mentality and setting up lives that operated within a 20 to 60 minute radius, I was driving across the country with all of my possessions and cat it tow. At a time when money was tight, I prioritized experiences over disposable pleasures like Starbucks, clothes and useless possessions. At a time when most young adults were climbing the bottom rungs of their chosen career path of stability and comfort, I was cliff diving into a path of entrepreneurship and it's resulting uncertainty and freedom.

I'm not saying I think there is anything wrong with being happy with where you live and living a simple life. I'm just saying that it's one thing to stay living in your home town, but it's another thing to NEVER leave it. I think people don't explore because they fear that life beyond their chosen boundary may reveal what they may be missing out on.

> *Lack of exposure to the outside world is the best way to ensure you never question the authenticity of your satisfaction with your life.*

I understand... humans are comfort-seeking beings. We want life to be pleasant. But, we try so hard to control the world around us that we limit it to only what we know. But, then within that narrow path of certainty we make ourselves miserable. The monotony of our mediocrity highlights every slight disruption. When every day is like the one before we seek the variety and novelty we crave through conflict, drama, or substance abuse.

> *Ask yourself, have you lived 20 years of life, or have you lived 1 year 20 times?*

If this sounds like you, I'm going to tell you the one thing you've been trying to avoid hearing... that you have a choice. Every day since the beginning of your chosen limitations, you have had a choice to be different. You have always had the option to cross the boundary, move it, or demolish it. And, every day going forward you will still have this choice. You can say yes to life. You can get in the car and drive farther than ever before. You can sit down and think about what you really want, but that you've told yourself you cannot have... or cannot go... or cannot do. You can spend your money differently. You can spend your time differently. You can stop hiding behind comfort and conformity and obligation.

And, if you're one of those people who loves your home town and wants to raise your kids and grow old where your roots are planted, do it! Every community needs established families to keep tradition and culture alive. But, don't do it out of fear or obligation.

Many people use this famous quote, by George A. Moore, as an excuse to stay put:

> *"A man travels the world over in search of what he needs and returns home to find it."*

To which I reply: *Sometimes*. More often, those who explore find themselves and what they need and love through exposure to people who think differently than they do, through finding beauty and meaning in experiences and places they didn't know existed. The truth is most people who leave don't return home. And those who do return home and find that, after all, what they always wanted was right where they began... they first had to "travel the world over" in order to realize it... or at least leave their state!

You've never heard anyone say "staying within a 1 hour radius was the greatest decision I ever made."

Take the risk. It's the only way you'll ever know that the only true risk is staying stuck where you are... in the prison of your own making. Only you hold the key. You always have. It's time to stop limiting yourself with imaginary boundaries.

You're free to go.

5: DE-CATASTROPHIZING (OVERCOMING WORRY)

This tool is great for talking yourself out of worrying or expecting the worst-case scenario, such as when you're making a big hairy deal about something. By looking at the facts of the situation it helps you reign in your exaggerated thinking and look more rationally at why this is happening.

Step 4.2 (D) Changing the Meaning You Assign (Evaluations)

What is the Catastrophe? Begins by identifying the catastrophe that you are worrying about.

Clearly state the predicted catastrophe:

How Terrible is It? Rate how terrible you believe this catastrophe will be on a scale from 0% (not so bad) to 100% (absolutely awful).

0%_____100%

How Likely is It? Has a similar event happened in the past? If so, how often has it occurred?

Make an educated guess of how likely it is to happen.

0%_____100%

What is the Worst that Could Happen? What is the worst-case scenario?

What is the best-case scenario?

What is the most likely outcome?

What are the Odds? If your worry did happen, what are the chances you'd be okay in:

1 week ____% chance | 1 month ____% chance | 1 year ____% chance

---

How Would You Cope? If this did happen, how would you cope with it?

If this has happened before, how did you deal with it?

What resources (people, skills, abilities, techniques, optoins) do you have that could help you handle it?

How Can You Reassure Yourself? Try to put yourself in a friend's shoes and think about what you would say to yourself about your worry.

What story could you tell yourself about the situation that would make you feel better about it?

After looking at the situation from this perspective, rate how terrible you believe this catastrophe will be?

0%_____100%

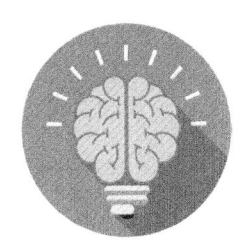

SECTION 10: STEP 4.3 (D): DISPUTING YOUR CORE BELIEFS

1: D = DISPUTING, PART 3—CORE BELIEFS

Go back and look at what you identified about your core beliefs in B. Using the Core Belief Identification Chart you identified which of the major musts that your beliefs fall under, which are APPROVAL, JUDGMENT, and COMFORT, as well as more specific beliefs. For each of the common core irrational beliefs we've addressed the TRUTH that counteracts the irrational belief. Use the document with the list of truths as a guide to help you shift your beliefs to be more rational.

Ask yourself the following questions for EACH of the irrational core beliefs you've identified:

1. What is the irrational core belief?
2. Why do you believe it? Why does this matter? (For example, you would ask yourself: why must I always get everything right? Why must everyone approve of me? Why does everyone have to love me?)

Note that there may not be a good, realistic answer to this question because the belief is illogical. Instead of seeking a real answer, ask yourself "what would happen if this didn't happen? Why would it matter? Continue to ask "why?" until you get to the core. Often the core answer will sound a lot like "because I would be worthless" or "because life wouldn't be worth living".)

- What is irrational or illogical about it?
- What evidence can you think of that proves this belief wrong?
- How could you re-write the belief so that it would be based on TRUTH and be rational?

And, again, looking at our example about the friend who passed you in the street without acknowledging you, your core belief was that you absolutely need to be loved and approved of by all people who are significant to you.

When you question this belief, you recognize that although being loved and approved of by everyone is highly desirable, they are not absolutely necessary.

You realize that not everyone is going to like you and you don't want to spend your whole life trying to be what other people want you to be.

2: CHALLENGING IRRATIONAL CORE BELIEFS

Once you've used the processes in steps AB and C and identified a core irrational belief, you can dispute it. This part is ultimately what the entire process has been leading up to because identifying the root of the problem—the core belief, rule, or demand—and shifting it to a rational belief is the key that unlocks lasting change.

This is exciting news, but you also need to keep in mind you may have spent years nurturing this belief and convincing yourself it is true. Some limiting beliefs don't let you rip them out by the root easily. It takes practice and persistence to change a core belief and develop an empowering belief that will serve you long term.

The best way to accomplish a belief shift is to wear it down through repetition. That is why this activity is meant to be done EVERY DAY. We recommend committing to this process daily for 14 days.

Set aside 10 minutes every day to identify a core irrational belief and ask yourself these questions. You may have identified a number of core beliefs during your other activities. You can also reflect on your day and identify any problems that came up and identify the core belief that lead to your disturbance.

Step 4.3 (D) Dispute Your Core Beliefs

When doing the activity, make sure you write down your answers. You can even record yourself instead. The reason this is so important is because your mind will try to pull you back into believing the old limiting belief. It has a habit of thinking that way and it will be easy to fall back into it. By writing it down, you can re-read your answers to remind yourself that the belief is irrational in those moments of weakness when it's tempting to believe it again.

Here are the questions:

1. What self-defeating irrational thought do I want to let go from my life and dispute?

2. Is my belief logical? Why or why not?

3. Is there evidence that disproves or counters this belief system?

4. Is there any evidence that shows this belief system to be true?

5. Is this belief productive? Where or what is it getting me?

6. Is it harmful to me?

7. What is the worst-case scenario if I do NOT get what I think I must (or if I get what I do NOT want)?

8. What positive things might happen if I do NOT get what I think I must have (or if I get what I do NOT Want)?

9. What is a rational belief that can replace the irrational one?

If you continue to practice questioning your core beliefs consistently, they will lose their power. Not only will your brain start to truly believe the new, rational belief, it will get better at spotting irrational beliefs in your every day life. You'll get so good at questioning your beliefs that you'll notice your emotions and behaviors throughout the day and automatically identify the core belief and challenge it right on the spot! Imagine how much heartache and stress this could save you!?

The last step is to be accountable! In order to reinforce your habit of disputing the irrational beliefs, determine a way you can reward yourself. For instance, you can choose an activity you enjoy, such as a hobby, socializing, or anything else you enjoy. Every day, after you complete this exercise, do the enjoyable activity as a way of rewarding yourself. This will help you associate disputing your beliefs with a positive emotional response, which helps reinforce the behavior.

Sometimes, in order to let go of a belief that isn't serving you, you need to find strong evidence that it is incorrect and strong evidence that the rational belief is correct.

3: CHANGING LIMITING BELIEFS

The Table Leg Method

Imagine your belief is like a tabletop and the evidence that supports your belief is like the table legs. You look at the evidence and make a conclusion—a belief about it. Just like with a table, if you knock enough legs out from under it the belief will collapse. You do this by creating doubt about your evidence or looking at it in a different way. Then, after you collapse the old, unwanted belief that makes you doubt yourself or your dream, you can use the same method to build up a new one. That's right, it works in reverse! If you determine a belief that is more empowering that you'd prefer, you can find evidence that SUPPORTS your new belief. Add at least 3 legs and the table will stand.

For example, if you believe that you are bad at math, you may have several reasons for this belief. First, it seems to run in your family. In fact, your mother said it's in her genes. This plants the first seed. Then, in 5th grade you got a math answer wrong when you were asked to do the math problem on the board in front of the class. It was embarrassing and rein-

Step 4.3 (D) Dispute Your Core Beliefs

forced your belief, making you thing "geeze, I guess mom was right!". Then, you failed the last two tests you took in your high school algebra class. You felt bad about it. Now the belief is stuck.

But, believing that you are innately bad at math will hold you back. First, because you expect to do poorly you'll be more nervous when you take math tests, you'll be less likely to try harder or practice since you believe you're simply unable to do math. You will unintentionally prove yourself correct. This is called a self-fulfilling prophecy. In the end, you'll avoid things that you might have enjoyed simply because you expect they'll involve math and you don't want to do it because you think you're bad at it. Maybe you love science, but you never pursued a career in science because you didn't think you could do the math. Maybe you wanted to start a business but didn't think you could handle the finances because of your math deficiency.

When we hold limiting beliefs, they hold us back from our potential.

The good news is even the more strongly held beliefs that hold up the overall belief can be undone. The key is to question the evidence we use to support it, remove the superglue, and find a new, more empowering belief to replace it with.

Before we begin, it's important to understand that when we're talking about limiting beliefs, we are not saying that the belief is FALSE. It may be true or based on things that really happened. But, whether it's true or false isn't the point. We're looking at beliefs that are either empowering or disempowering. They're either useful or harmful.

5 Step Process for Changing Limiting Beliefs

STEP 1: Identify a limiting belief you would like to change:

Make a list of all of the things you can think of that provide evidence (table legs) that support your belief (at least 3 pieces of evidence).

STEP 2: Identify an alternative belief that is more empowering: If you're having a hard time identifying a more empowering belief, ask yourself "what if I believed the opposite"? You want to choose a new belief that is believable. So, instead look for an IMPROVED belief. So, that could be "there is always opportunity in the market if you provide an exceptional product or service."

STEP 3: Unstick the emotional superglue: Sometimes we become emotionally attached to our limiting beliefs. We experience benefits or emotional payoffs for keeping our limitations around, which makes them sticky. It is like supergluing the table legs to the floor. So, ask yourself: what is the emotional payoff for holding onto this belief?

Be honest with yourself. Write down everything you can think of that may be an emotional or practical benefit.

Next, ask yourself: do these benefits outweigh the costs of keeping this limitation? __Yes __No

- If your answer is YES—that the emotional payoff is worth it—then you will most likely NOT be able to change this belief because you are too attached to it.

- If you answer is NO—the payoff is NOT worth continuing to be limited by this belief—well, then it's time to celebrate because you've just dissolved the superglue! You actually WANT to change, and that means it's time to start dismantling that table.

STEP 4: Create doubt by reframing your evidence: Like we said, you believe what you believe because you look at the evidence and come to a conclusion. But what if the evidence was wrong, incomplete, or you just weren't seeing it clearly? That would make you question your conclusion, and that's exactly the point of this step. For **each piece of evidence** you identified for your limiting belief, ask yourself the following questions:

- Could this be untrue?
- Is there more to the story?
- What is an alternative explanation?

The point is to question the evidence enough to create doubt. Some evidence will be harder to refute than others, but that's okay as long as you can knock out enough to leave less than 3 legs standing!

STEP 5: Find evidence to support your new belief:

Now we're gong to flip this around and build up the supporting evidence to solidify your new belief. Looking back at your desired belief, make a list of everything you can think of that supports this new belief. You only need a minimum of 3 but you want to create as many legs as possible so that this belief is way stronger than the old, limiting one.

With enough supporting legs, your new belief will stand. It might not be as strong as your old belief at first, but that is okay.

In many cases, the table legs that held up your old belief may have been really thick or really superglued because of the emotions tied to them. When thinking about evidence for your new belief, it may be harder to find emotionally-charged evidence, so you want to think of as many things as you can. The number of supporting legs will make up for the less powerful examples.

You've done it! You changed your limiting belief and replaced it with a new empowering belief! But that doesn't mean that the old limiting thoughts won't pop back up sometimes. You may need to remind yourself of this new belief multiple times, or even read it to yourself regularly, but through repetition you will be able to banish that limiting belief for good!

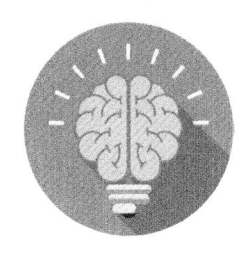

SECTION 11: STEPS 5 & 6 (E & F): DETERMINING THE DESIRED EFFECT, TAKING ACTION & CREATING CHANGE

1: E = NEW EFFECT

The fifth step in the ABCDEF process is E, which stands for the new desired effect.

In it's simplest terms, this step is about identifying what you want. The goal is to identify how you would prefer to feel, what outcomes you desire, and what changes you want to make to your behavior and actions. The way you will achieve this goal is to develop healthy, empowering RATIONAL beliefs.

By getting clear about your goals, you'll be ready to take the final step, which is to identify what further action needs to be taken.

In order to identify what you want, look back at what you've been working on in steps A through D.

Step 1: What is the activating event or situation you are focusing on?

- What were your automatic thoughts and assumptions about it?

- How did you feel (what were your unhealthy negative emotions)?

- Do you expect to be faced with a similar situation again in the future?

- How would you prefer to feel (what are the healthy negative emotions you could shift to)?

- How would you like to interpret the situation next time? How is this different from the first time?

- How would you have to think differently in order to feel the way you want to?

- How would making these changes impact you?

Step 2: What meaning did you assign to this event?

- In what way were you using dysfunctional thinking?

- How would you prefer to evaluate this situation?

- What would you like to believe that this means?

Steps 5 & 6 (E & F) Determining the Desired Effect, Taking Action & Creating Change

- What would you need to think or do differently to make this change?

- How would making these changes impact you?

Step 3: Which core irrational beliefs, musts or rules are being triggered by this situation?

- Which specific beliefs are at the core of what's going on here?

- How could you change each of these specific beliefs to be more rational?

- What do you want to believe?

- How would making these changes impact you?

Step 4: What were or are the emotional consequences of your beliefs?

- How would you prefer to feel about the situation?

Step 5: What were or are the behavioral consequences of your beliefs?

- What dysfunctional or unconstructive behaviors or actions have you or are you doing?

- How would you prefer to act or react? How could you behave more constructively?

Step 6: And finally, the last step is to identify your desired outcome.
- What are the negative, undesirable outcomes that have or will result from your feelings or actions?

- What is the outcome or result you would prefer to experience in this current situation?

- What is the outcome or result you would prefer to experience in the future if this situation was ever to happen again?

- What else that you haven't yet identified would you have to change, do, or do differently in order to create this desired outcome?

Looking back at our example about the friend who did not acknowledge you, you want to feel more confident. In order to feel more confident you would need to depend less on the approval of others for your sense of self worth., You want to believe your friend has a good reason for not acknowledging you, and so you would need to shift your perspective and assume that he did not notice you because he was distracted. And, you want to both reach out to your friend and continue to be social and develop strong friendships, and so you would need reach out, rather than withdrawing, and to develop a belief that even if this one friend did reject you, you are still a worthy person and a valuable friend.

2: F = FURTHER ACTION

The sixth and final step in the ABCDEF process is F, which stands for Further Action.

Steps 5 & 6 (E & F) Determining the Desired Effect, Taking Action & Creating Change

This last step is about determining what actions to take in order to accomplish your goals, which are the new effects you determined in step E. Ultimately, this means identifying what you will do or not do in order to avoid repeating the same reactions the next time you are faced with a similar situation. This step is so important because this is where you take responsibility for creating lasting change.

So, the questioning you're asking is "what do I need to do next?"

The best way to identify what steps to take is to look at an example, so let's finish with the example we've been using about the friend who didn't acknowledge you.

Your goals are to feel more confident, believe your friend had good intentions, reach out to your friend, and continue healthy relationships in general. So, here are several steps to take in order to accomplish these goals:

1. Choose a positive interpretation to commit to, such as assuming he did not see you because he was distracted. If you find yourself resisting this belief and switching back to the original interpretation, write yourself an affirmation and post it somewhere you can see it every day, such as on a mirror or in your phone. Affirm to yourself "I know that my friend cares about me because he is always kind and has been there for me. I am sure he didn't say hello because he was distracted and didn't see me." If you need to, write out a giant list of reasons why you believe this.

2. In order to feel more confident and feel less dependent on approval, plan time this week to review the "truth" statements in the corresponding belief under the Major Must #1 APPROVAL belief. Review them one time every day for a week. Also, complete the Changing Limiting Beliefs activity this week.

3. After completing the first two activities your mindset will be prepared to face the situation with a new perspective. So, at this point reach out to your friend through a phone call or even an email if a phone call is not possible. If you feel it would be helpful, decide ahead of time what you would like to say. If you wish to address that you saw them, find a way to say it that does not sound accusatory. For instance, you could say "Hey! I saw you by XYZ store the other day." And then allow them to respond, "Really? I didn't see you, when was that?"

4. And lastly, continue to develop healthy friendships by practicing challenging your irrational demands, including the ones about approval. Commit to practicing the processes in this program to identify and change your thoughts and beliefs. Schedule time on the calendar every day for 1 week in order to commit to improving your ability to direct your own thoughts, beliefs, emotions, and behaviors.
5. Another option to build confidence would be to do one thing each day that you would normally avoid doing for fear of judgment or rejection. By practicing being vulnerable to disapproval and finding that even if someone does disapprove, you are, in fact, still alive and perfectly worthy, it will help you get over your irrational fear.

So, now, for each of your goals, identify 2 to 4 action steps that you need to take to move toward your goal and when you will take them. Putting a timeline on your actions and putting them into your calendar or setting reminders will keep you accountable.

Goal	Action Steps	Timeline

3: OVERCOMING INDECISION PART 1: AUTOPILOT AND BEING STUCK

Indecision is a form of self-abuse. It's the ultimate form of giving away your power because it is our decisions that determine our destiny. One of the most important aspects of life that CBT can help with is decision making.

The first form of indecision is being on autopilot.

Some people don't make decisions at all. In fact, they aren't even aware of what they're doing. They blindly follow their impulses, or worse, their familial and cultural assumptions of how life "should" be. Many people respond to the stimulus of their environment with knee-jerk reactions, and their lives unfold on autopilot.

In the most extreme situations, their choices dramatically reduce their options, like choosing to drive recklessly and ending up in an accident that causes permanent disability or accidentally becoming pregnant at 15. Other decisions are more subtle, yet have lasting repercussions. Some people choose to settle for a practical career that they hate or take over the family business out of obligation. They may go to college for a degree they don't want or drop out because they don't know what they want. They may get married, have children, and climb the corporate ladder because it's what they're "supposed" to do. They may fall into habits or patterns that don't serve them or keep experiencing the same dysfunctional relationships over and over again. They may spend hours a day on social media or watching TV instead of working toward their dreams. They never stop to question their decisions and, if they do, it's often only after they're already suffering the consequences. They aren't aware that they could have had a totally different and, most likely, dramatically more epic life.

If you've been living your life on autopilot, this entire book is designed to help you become more aware of your thoughts and behaviors, which means you will be more conscious of the decisions you are, and are not, making. If you've been giving away your power, the exciting thing is now you know that you can take it back. Get in the habit of asking yourself what you want, as well as taking a moment to consider the outcomes or repercussions of the actions you take.

The second form of indecision is being stuck.

This happens when you recognize that you have a choice how to live, but you either cannot decide between your options or you cannot get yourself to move forward. You're stuck. There are 4 ways you can get stuck.

1. **Not Sure What You Want:** There may be times you don't take action because you're not sure what you want and so you do nothing. Like so many people, you might reach a decision point and then think and think and think, but never act. But, you are still making a decision because your indecision will ultimately lead to an undesirable outcome. By not deciding, you give away your power. Often, indecision means you wait too long and your choices are no longer available. Other times, it means you allow someone else to make the choice for you. The saddest form of indecision is when you know what you wanted but you let it slip away.
2. **Perfectionism:** One of the things that gets in the way for many people is perfectionism. Don't worry whether it's the "perfect" decision or whether it's the "right" direction. Making any decision in any direction gets things moving. For example, if you got in your car, turned on the GPS, and told it where you wanted to go, it may not initially lead you to the right direction if it does not recognize which way you are facing or if has not updated your location. However, as soon as your car starts moving it will get oriented and then tell you to go in the direction you need to go, even if it means turning around. The same thing happens when you take action in life. Getting started is the hardest part, but once you make a move—any move—it becomes easier to assess if you're going the right way and what steps to take to correct your path. See the next chapter where we'll talk about creating the spark to take that first step.
3. **Being Indecisive:** Are you not sure which option to choose? Try each one out. Taking even one step in one direction or another will help you gauge how you feel about it. If it is not possible to literally take a step or try it out, run through the possibilities in your mind. Imagine making the decision one direction. Imagine taking the first step.
    a. From there, what are the possible outcomes?
    b. How do I feel about each outcome?
    c. For each outcome, what are the possible next steps?
    d. Then, make the next decision and ask again…

See the Exposure Techniques chapter for a process that will help you use visualization to try out different options.
4. **Feeling Uncertain:** Are you avoiding making a decision to move forward on something because you're not sure how it will turn out? Uncertainty is a big road block for many people. It's normal to wish you could know how everything will turn out ahead of time, but the problem is that you can't. The solution is to take a small step. Test the waters. And in many cases, just simply do it! If you can't get yourself to make the leap, work through the steps of the process in your mind and check out the next chapter about overcoming inaction.

Next, we'll explore the 3rd form of indecision—those choices that are life changing.

4: OVERCOMING INDECISION PART 2: IRREVOCABLE CHOICES

Living on autopilot or getting stuck in indecision can hold you back and give your power away. Becoming aware of the thought processes that are keeping us from making a clear-minded decision, as well as getting clear about what we want, can help us make better decisions.

But the truth is that some decisions are harder than others.

The third form of indecision happens when the choices are irrevocable, meaning the repercussions of either choice are life changing. Sometimes we're faced with the terrifying reality that when we choose one path it means we will permanently eliminate our other options.

This is why so many people never make a leap into the unknown. They are paralyzed by fear—fear that they'll make the wrong decision. Fear they'll regret what they'll miss out on. They spend so long standing in trepidation that eventually they find themselves living the default life that their environment cultivates. The only difference between them and those who live on autopilot is that they ache inside for the dreams they never chose because they were aware of their options. But, it's too late—the ship has sailed. What they didn't realize is that whether they made that hard decision or not, a decision was made and something was lost. It's inescapable.

Some people run from the truth and avoid pain so much that they miss out on life completely.

When faced with such earth-shaking dilemmas, how do you choose?
- How do you choose whether or not to leave a marriage?
- How do you decide to quit your job and go back to school?
- How do you decide whether the freedom of entrepreneurship is worth the risk and uncertainty?
- How do you decide to move thousands of miles from your family and friends and miss out on important milestones?
- How do you decide whether or not to have a child?

Some life-changing decisions are easier than others.

We have found—through intensive firsthand experience, research into success and happiness, and experiences with our clients—that there are two stages we must go through to make those really hard decisions:
- Honesty
- Acceptance

HONESTY: We must be honest with ourselves about what we will lose, on both sides of our decision.

No matter what choices we make in life, we are destined to have a ghost ship— that contains all of the experiences, people, and options we did not choose. This ship is like an alternative version of our life that lives on without us, floating adrift in an infinite sea. I find this idea to be a great relief. We never have to let something go entirely because part of us holds it in our hearts forever.

The question, then, which of our options do we let sail away?

The following activity will help you really look at the benefits and consequences of each option.

What difficult decision are you facing right now?

What are your 2 choices?

1)

2)

Steps 5 & 6 (E & F) Determining the Desired Effect, Taking Action & Creating Change

Each of these options represent a life that you will either live, or not. Now, imagine you are choosing to live LIFE #1 and allowing LIFE #2 to drift out to sea.

- What are the positive, meaningful outcomes I'll experience if I choose LIFE #1?

- What are the negative, meaningful losses I'll experience because I did NOT choose LIFE #2?

Now, switch your choice around in your mind, allowing LIFE #1 to drift to sea, and imagine what it would be like.

- What are the positive, meaningful outcomes I'll experience if I choose LIFE #2?

- What are the negative, meaningful losses I'll experience because I do NOT choose LIFE #1?

Put it all on paper. Include everything you can think. Be brutally honest. And when you're ready, really ready to know your answer, sit down and ask the final question.

When you're 85 years old, which one would you regret NOT doing more?

At the end of this exercise, you'll be clear. Devastatingly clear. But that's okay because the weight will be lifted; the decision will be made. And, most importantly, you won't risk letting life pass you by, robbing you of your potential for greatness.

ACCEPTANCE: Next, you must accept the life that is truly yours to live and honor the one you are leaving behind.

You may never know what it was like to live the life you don't choose. It wasn't yours to live. But you'll be able to live the destiny you have created, knowing you made an empowered decision that honored who you truly are. Some of what you've left behind will fade from your mind completely; some will echo in your heart forever.

In order to create our beautiful lives, we have sent many possibilities, people and pieces of ourselves to live upon our ghost ships.

> "When I find myself facing another irrevocable choice, I am drawn to the sea. I stand on the shore with the waves lapping my feet. When I look to the horizon, I catch a glimpse of what looks like the shadow of a sail. I wiped away a tear, smile and waved gently to my phantom self and my life that I'll never know, knowing that no matter what I choose, part of me will always be adrift." —Natalie Rivera

Bon voyage.

5: OVERCOMING INACTION

Do you ever find yourself knowing what you need to do but just not able to get yourself to do it?

In order to understand why this happens, you need to understand activation energy. In chemistry, activation energy is the term used to describe the phenomenon that a tremendous amount of energy is needed in order to start any chemical reaction. Then, after this initial spark, a lot less energy is needed to keep it going.

Activation energy applies to human behavior too. Not having activation energy is why it can be so hard to get started, whether we're trying to go to the gym, make a phone call, or get out of bed.

Sometimes we need to create a SPARK to get us moving, that's big enough to keep us going. Other times we need to light a fire under our butt to remind us the big reason why we need to take this action.

So, the best strategy to create the SPARK that helps you take the first step toward ANYTHING is to use the 5-second rule.

(We have author and speaker Mel Robbins to thank for this gem!)

Why 5 seconds? Because your brain is wired to avoid risk and fear change. When the thought comes to your mind of the thing you want to do (but that you haven't done because of fear or resistance), if you wait more than 5 seconds your brain will try to talk you out of it, again. It will bring up all of the reasons you "shouldn't" do it, why it isn't a good time, what could go wrong, or the most clever one—"I don't feel like it." Well, unless what you're trying to do is 100% pleasurable (which it can't be, otherwise you wouldn't have to make yourself do it) chances are you will NEVER "feel like it". Now don't get me wrong, I'm not suggesting you should be forcing yourself to do things that truly aren't right for you. Don't make yourself suffer. Don't go against what your heart is telling you. But if your heart is telling you YES and your body still won't get in gear, give it a nudge!

By taking action, any small action, within 5 seconds you outsmart your own brain.

Here's how the 5 Second Rule works:

Anytime you have an idea that will better your situation, act IMMEDIATELY—within 5 seconds. Don't think, just do!

When the thought comes, start counting from 5 down to 1 and GET MOVING. There are 2 reasons that THIS IS THE KEY TO WHY THE 5 SECOND RULE WORKS!

1. It signals to your brain that there is an END to the countdown. If you counted from 1 to 5 you could keep going.
2. Counting distracts your mind, preventing it from thinking you out of it.

So, next time an idea comes to mind of something you know that if you did it you'd receive positive results, use the 5 second rule to DO IT NOW. When the thought comes, "I should make that phone call" count 5… 4… think of where your phone is… 3… 2… reach for your phone… 1… dial the number.

There are so many uses for this! Before I had ever heard of the idea of the 5 second rule, I used this immediate action strategy on MYSELF to get myself to stop procrastinating doing the dishes.

Then, when it worked, I used it on everything! I'd notice my resistance and use that as a trigger to act IMMEDIATELY.

Another excellent use of the 5 second rule is to start a new habit! Breaking an old habit requires you to replace it with a new habit. You can use the 5 second countdown to start the new ritual that will interrupt the old behavior pattern.

6: EXPOSURE TECHNIQUES FOR OVERCOMING FEAR AND RESISTANCE

Often the best way to overcome anything that you resist or are afraid of is to expose yourself to it in a way that gently gets you used to it. You can accomplish this gradual desensitization effect both mentally and in real life.

Imagery Based Exposure

The mind does not know the difference between reality and what is happening in the mind. Whether a situation is happening or you're imagining or remembering it, the brain reacts the same by producing the neurochemicals that make you feel an emotional response. This means that if you are afraid of something, whether it's public speaking, bringing up a difficult conversation, or riding in an airplane, you can use visualization to practice exposure mentally. This tool can also be used to practice a new skill or make a life change. Change can be scary, so using visualization is one way to overcome resistance by getting used to the experience ahead of time. You can work through the intimidating parts in your mind and play out all of the different options so that you know ahead of time how you want to react when it comes time for the real experience. Skills can also be practiced using visualization because imagining executing the skill or steps in great detail helps the brain create a habit of thought. Then, when you take the steps in real-life, it doesn't feel new, it feels like you've done this before.

Regardless of the situation you wish to expose yourself to mentally, determine what the experience would look like. Would there be steps to take? What would be going on around you? Who would be there? Sit down, close your eyes, and imagine the experience from start to finish. Imagine every step in great detail. When you experience a negative emotion of resistance or fear, observe how it feels. Ask what you are thinking about the situation that is making you feel that way. Ask yourself what you would want the experience to look like in order for you to feel more comfortable with it. Then, continue imagining the experience going well. Imagine yourself feeling comfortable and content. You can even add fun or relaxing elements to the scene if you want, such as music or color. Imagining the situation with these added elements helps program the mind to expect to feel good when the situation happens in real life. You may need to do this activity several times until you can go through the entire process feeling good.

Situation Exposure Hierarchies

Another way to gradually expose yourself to something in a way that overcomes resistance and fear is to take baby steps. First, identify something, or multiple things, you are avoiding. Then, identify what steps or actions involved in this situation that you are feeling resistant to doing. This could be having a conversation, committing to something, taking an action, making an investment, etc. For each of the aspects that you feel resistance about, rate them on a scale of 1 to 10, 10 being extremely high resistance or fear. Put the different aspects or steps in order based on their score. Then, start taking the steps with the lowest level of resistance first, working your way up to the more difficult steps. Doing this builds confidence, and because the smaller tasks are already out of the way, you will feel less overwhelmed and will build your way to the more difficult steps.

Another way to use exposure hierarchies is the exposure ladder. We've included a bonus chapter, which is coming up next, that shows how to use an exposure ladder to overcome fear of public speaking. The process applies to anything you want to overcome.

Play the Script Until the End (the Worst Case Scenario)

Another great process for overcoming fear and resistance is to actually face the fear itself. The way you do this is to imagine the situation and play the script all the way to the end, which would be the worst case scenario that you are afraid of. The benefit of doing this is that you can see what it would actually be like without having to experience it in real life. It gives you a safe place to see how it would feel and determine how you would cope with it. See the De-Catastrophizing chapter for a great activity.

7: IDENTIFYING WHAT YOU WANT

So, what do you want? If you're like most people, this is surprisingly difficult to answer. Most people are so inundated with messages from their parents, peers, and society of what they "should" want that their true desires are drowned out. Plus, even if they've held dreams and desires in the past, their life experiences have lead them to believe that what they want is not possible, and so they stop allowing themselves to want it. They tell themselves "I can't have that" and it hurts to want something they cannot have, and so they stop thinking about it. They give it up. They settle.

But, the good news is that dreams can never die—deep down you know what you want. It tugs at you from within, but you may be so used to ignoring it that you no longer notice.

Forgotten Dreams

What do you REALLY want? Answer this without allowing other people's opinions or beliefs to limit you. Answer this without thinking about limitations—imagine for a moment that money is not an issue and that whatever that is currently blocking you is magically taken care of.

What do you not allow yourself to want? What are things you wanted, desired or dreamed about that at some point you decided you could NOT have and so stopped wanting them?

This could have been in childhood or adulthood. You may not have allowed yourself to think about these desires in a long time. For each one, ask yourself if this is something that you STILL want. If not, cross it out and let it go. Circle any desires that you feel a strong emotional reaction to when you think about them.

Identifying What You Do NOT Want

For many people it's easier to identify what they do NOT want than what they DO want. When asked what they want, many people respond "not this!" So, to start, simply make a list of the things you know for sure you do NOT want in your life. These can be things that USED to be in your life that you never want to experience again. They can be things CURRENTLY in your life that you would like to stop. They can be things you are simply certain you never want in your FUTURE.

Once you know what you do NOT want, it will help you identify what

Steps 5 & 6 (E & F) Determining the Desired Effect, Taking Action & Creating Change

you DO want. Ask yourself, "What is the opposite of what I don't want?"

I do NOT want:	I DO want:

Getting More Specific

You have determined some things you want and don't want. You have determined the roles, beliefs and ego states that have influenced your life story and the new perspectives you can now take of them. Now, it is time to delve into greater detail about what you WANT your life to be. You can always add to this activity later, as you learn more about your desires. Later you will rewrite the story itself, but here you are asking yourself what you want in your life and why.

AREA	WHAT DO I WANT?	WHY DO I WANT IT?
Home		
Partner/ Relationship		
Family		
Career		
Leisure		
Money		
Health		
Other		

"Yes, I want more of this!"

Once you begin asking yourself about what you want, you'll find yourself noticing more and more things that make you think, "yes, I want this!" It's okay if you're still not sure what you want. Allow your desire to grow over time. Throughout your day, simply notice whether you like or dislike certain things, people, situations or experiences.

Say, "Yes, I want more of this!" to the things you like.

Say, "No, thank you." to the things you do not like. Saying "thank you" acknowledges that you appreciate the ability to identify what you don't want because it helps you know more clearly what you DO want.

Digging Deeper into "Why"

Now we're going to ask you to dig deeper into the answers you provided in the "why" column. This is important because only if you have a **big enough reason** will you be committed to creating lasting change. And, the only way your reason to change your life will be big enough is if you understand your core reasons. Below is an example that will help illustrate the point.

A student in one of our classes once told us, "I can't wait to go home and start using these efficiency techniques to make my work more effective and productive" And so we asked, "Well, why do you want to be more productive?" The student said that it would help her to get a promotion at work. We asked her why she would want a promotion and she said "So I can get a raise." So we asked again, "Why do you want a raise" and she said "Because I need the money to buy a larger home". So we asked "Why?" and she says because I want my mother and sister to move in with me". "Why?" "Because it has been our dream to own a big house together and live together as a family."

To which we responded, "Good, NOW you have identified what you really want. It's a large house with your family living with you. You don't really want to be more efficient. What you want is the experience of having your family living with you."

Look at the reasons you wrote in the "getting more specific" activityin the "why" column, and ask yourself the following questions:
- Why does this matter to me?
- Why?
- How would it make me feel?

Steps 5 & 6 (E & F) Determining the Desired Effect, Taking Action & Creating Change

- What would happen if I didn't have, do, or be this?
- Why does that matter?
- Why?

Keep probing and asking yourself until you get to the core of the issue.

In some cases, you will find that your deeper motive is a specific desire, like in the example above. However, often the core motivation beneath your desire is actually an emotional state that you wish to experience. In fact, everything we want is because we believe it will make us *feel* the way we desire: good, or at least *better*.

Get Other People Out of Your Head

Lastly, consider if any of the things you "want" are truly only because you think you "should" want them. It's easy to unknowingly adopt other people's dreams. Get other people's voices and beliefs out of your head... then take a final look at your desires and confirm that this is TRULY what you want.

8: THE BRAIN SCIENCE OF VISUALIZATION

Professional athletes and performers almost all use visualization because it works. The body does not know the difference between what is happening and what we imagine or remember. When a runner visualizes a race, while attached to electrodes, the exact same sequence of brain activity is observed as when the runner is physically racing.

If you imagine eating a juicy lime and tasting its sour juice, your mouth will salivate because your mind has tricked your body. The same is also true if you visualize yourself failing or losing.

According to research using brain imagery, visualization works because neurons in our brains, those electrically excitable cells that transmit information, interpret imagery as equivalent to a real-life action. When we visualize an act, the brain generates an impulse that tells our neurons to "perform" the movement.

In 2004, the Cleveland Clinic conducted a study on mental exercises and the impact that it has on strength (in participants' fingers and arms). They separated people into three groups and had them follow a protocol for 12 weeks. One group did the physical exercises. One group visualized doing the exercises. The last group did nothing. At the end they re-tested their strength. When it came to finger strength the group that physically did the exercises had a 53% increase in strength, the ones that visualized it had an increase of 35%, and the ones that did nothing had no significant change.

> *It is incredible to think that your thoughts are so powerful that simply visualizing exercising your finger can significantly increase your strength, without any physical movement.*

They also found that arm strength increased by 13% through visualization alone. If your mind can do that, what else can it do for you that you may not be tapping into?

Another study looked at the brain patterns of weightlifters, both when they were lifting hundreds of pounds and when they were only imagining lifting. They found the brains were activated similarly by the actual and imaginary lifting. Many studies have found mental practices are almost as effective as physical practice, with the greatest benefit being combining the two. For example, another study at Cleveland Clinic, conducted by exercise psychologist by Guang Yue, compared "people who went to the gym with people who carried out virtual workouts in their heads". The gym-goers had a 30% increase in muscle strength, while the participants who exercised only mentally increased their strength by 13.5%, which is nearly half the benefit with none of the work! This actual strength from imaginary exercise remained for 3 months following the mental training.

This is important! What we imagine and visualize ourselves experiencing: a) impacts our brain and body and b) creates real outcomes in our lives.

First, think about what you're doing to yourself every time you re-live those old yucky memories and replay them over and over again in your mind? You're right, you actually ARE reliving them! This is why you can continue an argument with your boss or spouse hours after the real one happened, or days before you actually confront them, yet you feel the same rush of angry emotions flood your body. Yup, your body think's it's real. Stop it!

Second, think about how powerful it would be if you used the new-found knowledge about how your mind and emotions work deliberately, in order to create positive emotions through positive imaginings? Imagine if you mentally created the future life you want to live and rehearsed how it would feel, what it would look like, who you would be, and what it would be like to live your dreams NOW in your mind? You can, because your mind doesn't know the difference, remember? Why not go there now?

That's exactly what you're going to do next.

9: CREATE A VISION OF YOUR FUTURE

Looking back at everything you've learned about your irrational thinking and the beliefs that were holding you back, we hope that by now you can see that you have more potential than you ever could have imagined! You are the proud owner of the world's most powerful machine, and now you have a better idea of how to use it!

After banishing your limiting beliefs and reigning in your monkey mind, you can envision a future for yourself with more clarity and hope than ever before. Now, you can dream your dreams and feel confident that you have the mindset and tools to make the necessary changes within yourself to get there. Go you!

So, the last exercise in this book is to create a vision of your future! Look back at what you identified that you want in your life in Section 11.7. When writing your vision, use the desires you identified and write your story of your future self as if it's happening now.

With your newfound understanding of where your thoughts, beliefs and desires come from, you will be able to create a vision of your future from a place of genuine desire, not irrational demands and musts. You'll dream your dreams without being limited by "shoulds". When your negative self-talk pops-up, you will know what to do, and you will have the ABCDEF process and other tools from this Human Mind Owner's Manual to give your monkey mind a banana when it needs one!

When writing your vision, follow the same 4 P's rules from the positive thinking and affirmations chapter:
- Personal (I, Me statements)
- Passion (put emotion into it)
- Present (as if it's already happening, not future or past)
- Positive (avoid words like "not" or "don't")

Most importantly, write your vision from a growth mindset perspective, knowing that whatever it is you dream to do, you can learn, grow and improve in order to get there.

Pandora's Box has been opened. You've taken the Red Pill. You cannot un-know what you've learned! But, your journey has just begun. Now that you've looked at the hand you've been dealt from a new perspective, we hope you can see that you really can have, do or be whatever it is you want if you master the power of your mind.

Your Vision:

MEET THE AUTHORS:

Joeel & Natalie Rivera

Joeel and Natalie Rivera are freedom junkies and prolific content creators who have launched over a dozen business. They have also been coaching, speaking, writing, and teaching for more than a decade.

Through their online education company Transformation Academy, they empower life coaches, INDIEpreneurs and transformation junkies to create a purpose-driven life and business and master the power of their mind so they can create their destiny.

Joeel is a former psychology professor with a Master's Degree in Counseling and Education and has been studying happiness for his dissertation for a Ph.D. in Psychology.

After almost losing it all in 2014 due to a sudden illness after traveling overseas, they converted their workshops, coaching and training programs into online courses. Today, they've created more than 85 online courses, taken by more than 750,000 students from 200 countries (at the time of this writing).

They believe that entrepreneurship is the ultimate form of empowerment. They believe in turning pain into purpose. And, they believe in the democratization of education and, therefore, make their programs available at a price that is within reach of students worldwide.

WWW.TRANSFORMATIONACADEMY.COM

TAKE THE ONLINE COURSE!

Learn directly from instructors Joeel & Natalie!

This book covers content taught in two of Transformation Academy's best-selling online courses! Enroll in both of these interactive video-based training programs for free! Plus, download printable worksheets!

ENROLL FOR FREE!
Visit: https://www.transformationacademy.com/ownersmanual
Use coupon code: *ownersmanual*

If you are a life coach (or want to be), enroll in the **CBT Life Coach CERTIFICATION and/or REBT Mindset Life Coach CERTIFICATION** programs, which includes all content covered in this book, plus additional training for how to use these tools and processes with clients!

UPGRADE FOR ONLY $97 EACH!
(That's 50% off!)
Visit: https://www.transformationacademy.com/ownersmanual
Use coupon code: *mindsetcoach*

PLUS, **save 50%** on all of our 60+ other courses!

Use coupon code: **ownersmanual50**

Printed in Great Britain
by Amazon